The

Disciplined

Heart

RUTH C. IKERMAN

The
Disciplined
Heart

New York • ABINGDON 🄰 PRESS • *Nashville*

THE DISCIPLINED HEART

Copyright © 1964 by Abingdon Press

Library of Congress Catalog Card Number: 64-19347

SET UP, PRINTED, AND BOUND BY THE
PARTHENON PRESS, AT NASHVILLE,
TENNESSEE, UNITED STATES OF AMERICA

Dedicated to

Christian women everywhere as typified by the busy and beloved workers who call my mother their own *"Mom Percival"*

Preface

Much is being said about the need for physical fitness in the space age, but little has been done to help us develop hearts which are fit to solve the problems of today's world.

This little book has been written to try to help the average woman meet her special problems in home, church, community, and nation by the exercise of her heart through certain spiritual disciplines.

This word "discipline" comes from the same root word as "disciple." Therefore these ideas are a simple extension of our wish to be good disciples as we live our busy lives through the quickly changing months of each passing year.

7

Twelve chapters relate to these yearly months, and each closes with specific suggestions for seasonal action. Others deal with definite life situations. There is a theme Bible verse for encouragement, a prayer, and also a human interest anecdote introducing the problem and suggesting an answer.

May each of us be blessed by God as we try to act on the sacred obligation: "Keep thy heart with all diligence; for out of it are the issues of life."

Ruth C. Ikerman

Contents

Disciplines
to Practice Every Month of the Year

Disciplines
to Help You Solve Specific Problems

*Disciplines to
Practice Every Month
of the Year*

1

*January Verse for the Month: "Trust in him
at all times; ye people, pour out your heart before him:
God is a refuge for us."*—Ps. 62:8

Days That
Have Never Been Used

On that busy January afternoon we almost
missed the quiet knock at the front door. There stood
the tiniest boy we had seen in a long time, barefoot
despite the seasonal rain. In his hand he held a rolled-
up piece of paper which was the familiar color of one
of the calendars sold as a benefit in our part of
America.

One edge was slightly torn, I saw at first glance,
and I realized that somebody must have discarded

13

this calendar. In our house we had finally learned to write the new digit for the fresh year, and had destroyed last year's calendars, and were enjoying the pictures on the new ones.

The lad held out the calendar in his hand and seemed blissfully unaware of any defects. He offered it proudly and hopefully. "Lady," he said, "here is a calendar with lots of perfectly good days that have never been used."

Would I like to buy it? His manner implied that if I didn't, probably nobody else would. Surely this was the last chance to purchase such a bargain.

"These days have never been used at all," he told me earnestly, as if this should settle the matter for me. And it did. What wouldn't I give for some extra days which had never been used at all, I thought in my heart, as I went for my purse and the proper change for the price he asked for his calendar.

How his face brightened as I handed him the money. He galloped down the sidewalk, and turned around at the street's edge to call back, "I found this calendar down at the dump."

This became my favorite calendar, for I worked hard to try to make sure that none of the days ever went back to the junk pile.

What a wonderfully happy time I had trying to redeem the discarded calendar. For it reminded me vividly of the great blessing of receiving anew each year from the hand of God the gift of days that have never been used.

All of us receive such days, but we so often take them for granted. Indeed, we do not think of them as "new" at all. When we are asked what we are doing, we frequently reply, "just the same old things."

Yet the new days offer new opportunities for service, a fresh chance to open our eyes wide to the beauties of our own neighborhood, the courage being expressed daily by friends as they carry their own burdens silently and bravely.

Somebody discarded days of this calendar thinking he already had enough means of keeping track of time, and we often throw away the days themselves just as lightly. Yet for each of us this might be the beginning of the last year we are to know on this earth. We know from the losses in previous years that without doubt this is the last year for some of our friends and acquaintances or leaders in our churches and communities. Perhaps it is this which adds the poignancy to the carefree greeting, "Happy New Year," for there is uncertainty as to its length, and the quality of its experiences is hidden in the days ahead.

One thing which makes each day a blessed experience while it is being lived and which adds to its positive weight in eternity is an awareness that this day does come from God. In his great democracy he grants each day anew to each individual, a day at a time. Nobody can receive a day in advance of its timing, and nobody can hoard a day to spend tomorrow. The one thing which the individual has in his power to do with a day is to throw it away "at the dump," or to redeem it through joyful use of each minute of every hour.

Each of us has a special opportunity in home, church, and community, to give the widest possible value to the great gift of days which have never been used. Sometimes we yearn wistfully for the ability to make the maximum use of our days. Certain simple disciplines can help us achieve in our hearts a happy feeling that we are making the right use of time. Practiced faithfully they will become a habit of living, which will add to our usefulness. Here are two disciplines to try out in January to help set the tone for the entire New Year.

Discipline for Inner Growth: Spend five minutes in the morning and five minutes at noon, quietly thinking about the gift of this day, realizing that it comes from God. In the stillness, he will make you more and more aware of ways to spend the time on those you love as his representatives. Learn to say, "Thank you, God, for the blessings of this day," in a final evening prayer as you go to bed. This has the psychological effect of preparing your heart to receive a better tomorrow.

16

Discipline for Outer Action: Each day have the satisfaction of doing one thing you have previously thought your busy schedule could not possibly include time for enjoying. This may mean just taking a walk around the house to admire or plan a garden, baking a different cake recipe, writing a letter to an old friend, or telephoning a new acquaintance. From these personal pleasures will come an increasing vision of your part in group adventures such as your church circle, club section, or community agencies. Your private schedule will adjust to such spiritual responsibilities when it knows that now you are determined to gain maximum value from the rich gift of each day that has never been used.

Prayer: God of eternity, we thank thee for giving us this small portion of endless time to use today in our own homes and places of employment. Accept our gratitude for this generous and great gift. Forgive us for being stingy in the way we have previously shared our days with others. Help us now to accept each new day gladly, as we become increasingly aware of the joys of using time effectively for thee. Amen.

2

February Verse for the Month: "And thou shalt love the Lord thy God with all thine heart, and with all thy soul, and with all thy might."—Deut. 6:5

I Love You, Too

While I was visiting in the home of young parents, the mother told me that the little son had a game he played each night. He would go around the family circle, pausing in front of each member and guest. Then he would say, "I love you."

Properly advised in advance, I was to watch and share in this happy ritual. His face shining with a radiant smile and his blue eyes alert, he stopped before my chair, looked me over carefully, and said, "I love you."

It was such a wonderful moment for me, being included in the intimate circle of this modern family, that I blurted out the first thing which came from my own heart, "I love you, too."

He sat down on the floor and looked up at me with a glance of incredulous surprise. "You do?" he asked me earnestly, with joy on his face I shall long remember.

Plain to all in the room was the fact that until this moment it had not occurred to him that somebody could love him back. He had supposed that loving was the means by which the little people cultivated the favor of the big, grown-up people in his life.

His delight at being told he was loved back was a marvel to behold. Yet surely he had always been the most loved person in that room, being surrounded by adoring grandparents, older aunts and uncles, and cousins, as well as by his proud parents.

It was a wonderfully revealing moment when he found out that somebody could love him back. His reaction illustrated vividly what happens in every life, regardless of age, when the discovery is made that loving is not a one-way-street.

To be loved back is one of the most marvelous experiences in any lifetime, and it is always the assurance in the heart of the Christian. At the center of our faith is the verse, "For God so loved the world, that he gave his only begotten son, that whosoever

19

believeth in him should not perish, but have everlasting life" (John 3:16).

Some people find it hard to accept this verse partly because they have not yet learned to allow other people to love them. They set up walls of defenses against those within their own homes, the neighbors next door, and the friends seen in clubs and church, which make it almost impossible for those outside to break through into the heart which in loneliness has shut itself against overtures made in love.

Once this initial barrier is overcome, there is the next step of learning how to love others in return. From here it is a natural outgrowth to come to respect institutions and to express love by contributions to the agencies which care for others through civic concern and intelligent compassion.

Those who minister in such departments of government or church-related agencies testify to the power of love in solving problems. In dealing with a delinquent boy, the case worker counseled "If this youth had known love from his parents, he would not be so hungry to get attention through misdeeds." The parents had not expressed their love verbally for fear of sounding sentimental.

In all such cases the experts counsel that it is far better to err on the side of being repetitious with what should be obvious than to let loving words go unsaid. This is particularly true where marital problems are involved. Often the halting or faltering words "I love you" will revive memories of happier days in courtship and serve as a basis for a solution of a current problem which seems to be leading a marriage to divorce courts.

One reason why such a statement of love is not made more readily is that it places the individual in the spot of being vulnerable in case the love is rejected. So we all need to remember the childlike attitude of the small boy in the family circle who dared to say to each one, "I love you." Something of his loving attitude expressed by adults will keep alive the agencies which minister to the aged and mission projects in war-torn portions of God's world. The overwhelming joy of being loved back is reserved for those who make the first contact by offering their own love. February, the month of valentines and heroes who loved their country, is a good month in which to learn disciplines of loving.

Discipline for Inner Growth: Search your memory for the person you have loved the most in your lifetime and write down the name, whether it be mother, husband, child, minister, or teacher. Opposite it place the name of the person you find it most difficult to love. Then write down the reason why there is this great difference in your love for these two people. This will clear your mind of haziness and enable you to start extending your already established love toward those who are currently unloved.

Discipline for Outer Action: This month you have a choice of disciplines and may alternate them, depending on mood and inclination. Disciplines do not have to be hard and harsh, for you can learn to make them fun as they fit into your schedule. The first outer discipline involves making sure that someone dear to you knows of this fact anew—through your preparation of a special dish in the kitchen to please his palate, the writing of a long-delayed note of thanks for some courtesy or kindness, or the lending of a book showing concern for the individual's taste. The second discipline is harder, for it means speaking to someone you cordially dislike. You must make the beginning toward loving by saying "Good morning" in a civil tone, even though you would rather cross the street or sit in a different pew in church.

Prayer: God of love, who cared enough about us to come to earth in the human form of thy son, grant us a fresh awareness of the power of love in problem solving. Show us how to make love practical. Let us know the healing joy of love as a soothing balm for the heartaches of hatred. Amen.

3

March Verse for the Month:
"Thou shalt not hate thy brother
in thine heart."—Lev. 19:17

First
Cleanse the Inside

One of the dreams shared by most women is that of having a beautifully appointed kitchen, complete with modern equipment for baking birthday cakes for the family. Sometimes it means saving a long time to afford the new stove, glossy paint for walls, and a bookshelf to hold cookbooks and the blue pitcher from great-grandmother's farm home.

When plans do materialize, it is a joy to keep the

23

room clean, and put fresh curtains at the window looking out on the garden's blossoming border. So it was a real disappointment when my own new kitchen began to have a stale odor.

No matter what new plastic polish was used on the tile, the floor seemed permeated with dirt. Change of scouring powder for the sink made no difference, nor use of cleansers poured into the trap to remove any waste fats accumulated. The repairman was called to see if there was stagnant water gathered below the washing machine and dishwasher, or leaking gas from furnace pipes.

Nobody thought to consider the shiny white refrigerator with a freezer compartment. It looked so clean and so self-assured. Finally, my husband took the situation in hand and removed the bottom panel and investigated. Inside was a pan about which the seller and service man had failed to inform us. We did not dream that the new mechanical style held to the drip pan which had been used to catch drops on the earliest ice chest.

Carefully my husband removed this hidden pan, filled now with stagnant water whose stench was almost unbearable when taken from behind the metal door. We emptied the water outdoors and with a hose washed the pan and left it in the good clean sun to be sterilized, and wiped by the winds of the sky.

That pan had gone unnoticed and unemptied during the time we had owned the refrigerator. It had caught the overflow of anything spilled and useless. There in the pan the offending refuse had begun to penetrate the entire room and spoil the home itself. No amount of scrubbing on the outside would have changed the aroma, or truly cleaned our beloved kitchen. Now with a cleansed pan it is once more a joy to work at family chores. The scent of orange blossoms comes in through the opened window, and the kitchen sends back its own perfume of warm gingerbread and cinnamon apples.

Remembering the neglected pan, I have wondered if there is something in my own life which hinders the fragrance of fellowship from permeating the days and years. Is there a hidden tray of resentment, a deep trough of old remembered sorrows, a section filled with hatred and criticism? We thrust these back because we know they would hinder necessary daily action, but they remain in the background to fester in the personality.

Any such debris needs to be taken from its dark hiding spot and brought to the light and thoroughly cleansed. Clutched too closely to the heart for too long, the musty odor of bitterness clings to the personality, and repels those who long to come forward with precious bouquets of friendship.

All the useless energy of going through the motions of keeping the outside clean will do no lasting good until the inside has first been cleansed. Jesus said, "Cleanse first that which is within the cup and platter,

25

that the outside of them may be clean also" (Matt. 23:26). He asked his followers to do this first, and so be ready for constructive action in keeping with his command, "Fill ye up then the measure of your fathers." (Matt. 23:32.)

Daily we have a fresh chance to let go of all that hinders the development of loving concern, by clearing our hearts and offering the faults to him. Then by his grace we can be restored to service and creative happiness. There is no better time than March, the month of housecleaning and inventory for tax purposes, to take stock of the dirt which has accumulated in the heart, and the negative attitudes which need to be written off as bad debts. Much progress can be made in March by concentrating on disciplines to cleanse the heart of impurities.

Discipline for Inner Growth: Probably you already know the factor causing the dust of discouragement to color your daily attitude, whether this is a loss through death or a betrayal by someone you long had trusted. Don't be afraid to look now into the dark corners of your mind. Open the shades of your life wide and see where the dust has settled the deepest over daily duties. You may even find "little gray kittens" of lint under your dreams, where big chunks of disillusionment have seemingly settled in for good. There is just one way to get rid of them, and that is by getting down on your knees and asking God to remove all stains. Keep them from accumulating again by resolving to live well in the present and by putting the dead past behind you.

Discipline for Outer Action: Confession is an all but outmoded technique in this busy life. Sometimes this is the only way to cleanse the heart. If there is someone you have wronged, whose face continues to come between you and happy action, then there remains this pathway to setting the matter straight. Either talk to that person face to face or send a brief note asking to have the past canceled out, so you both may live better in the future. Probably the other person is crippled and inactive also as a result of the hindrance of your critical resentment. If there is no one in your life blocking your growth, then thank God and keep busy on constructive projects.

Prayer: Dear Heavenly Father, help us lift our feet and wade out from any stagnant waters of regret or rebellion. Guide our steps to the still waters beside green pastures where we may receive fresh strength. Then lead us to channels of usefulness where we may offer the water of life to others who need thy love expressed in daily acts of kindness. Amen.

4

*April Verse for the Month: "He hath made
everything beautiful in his time: also he hath set
the world in their heart, so that no man can find out
the work that God maketh from the beginning
to the end."—Eccl. 3:11*

A Morning for Daffodils

In our garden there are hosts of daffodil
bulbs, hidden during most of the year, but which send
their golden treasure above the dusty earth for our
enjoyment each springtime. So I did not want to leave
for an early vacation, for it was the time for the blossoming of the daffodils.

Traveling across country from the west coast to
the east, I saw little houses with white curtains at
the window, and women working in their gardens

or hanging washing on the line. The daffodils border-
ing their walks reminded me of those left at home
for my neighbors to pick, and I felt a tug of home-
sickness.

This was complicated by a terrific storm encountered
in the south which sent us to a motel near world-
famous gardens. When the rains finally abated and
the sun came out, my husband suggested that we take
an extra hour to see what, if anything, was left of
the nearby gardens. Guides pointed out the towering
azaleas in all shades, beautiful camellia trees, their
pink reflection showing in the blue of the lake surrounded by its grassy, green plots, and flowering trees
contrasting with gray-green moss.

Here was beauty calculated to let me forget the
tiny garden with the well-beloved daffodils at home.
Then the guide rounded a turn and before me was
a solid planting of golden daffodils. The bright sun,
coming after the storm, was so blinding it dazzled my
eyes at is was reflected by the flowers. Any way I
turned on the path the daffodils followed me. Slowly
I made a complete circle until I stood in the center
of this planting, and daffodils were everywhere my
eye could look, blotting out my footsteps.

Surrounded by the flowers I love best, and which
I had thought were left behind in my own little
garden, I glimpsed a truth about future living and
trusting God. Silently I said to myself, "I hope I can
remember this morning when I must watch a loved

29

one leave his earthly home, with the daffodils not yet in bloom."

For I would never have seen this beauty if we had not left our own little house with its daffodils safely hidden in the sod. It was impossible to stay and go at the same time, much as my heart might want to do so. By leaving behind for others the daffodils which I had planted, it had somehow been granted me to come upon these, planted by others, which were destined for my own enjoyment.

It was a morning for daffodils, blessed by the sun, washed by the rain, kept by the eternal stars. It is a morning to which I return in thought many times as the year wears away. But never do I see these flowers so clearly as I do during Easter week. For immortality must burst upon us something like that morning in the garden when the blossoms completely surrounded us.

So each season I plant a few more daffodils in my little garden at home, in memory of the abundance of the beauty seen in travel, a glimpse of the possibilities inherent in another springtime. Often the bouquets go to someone who has suffered a loss, and who is involved deeply with sorrow and regret or remorse. In the bottom of the container or the foil surrounding the stems, I try to place a brown bulb for the friend to plant in her own garden.

Just seeing the stark simplicity of a thin layer of skin over the heart of the bulb, and comparing this with the fragile beauty of the completed flower, offers a striking lesson in what is changed through the magic of growth. The bulb pursues its intended course through death in the ground to life in new surroundings beneath the blue of the sky, nourished by the sunshine.

Sometimes the planting of the bulb is the first act of faith and a simple beginning toward the restoring of hope following the loss of one who represented life to the survivor immersed in sorrow. How I long to comfort her by more adequately describing the wonder of the massing of daffodils into one giant gem of beauty, glistening in glory with the drops of the storm dripping off, just as teardrops disappear with new activities. A morning for daffodils reminds us of disciplines which the heart can follow to help bridge the gap between death and Easter's golden morning.

Discipline for Inner Growth: Open your Bible and read aloud, "The Lord is my shepherd," pausing after each verse of the twenty-third psalm. Think of these words as relating to you and your own loved ones. When you have finished the period of meditation, repeat the affirmation from Ps. 116:9, "I will walk before the Lord in the land of the living."

Discipline for Outer Action: Find the one closest to you who has been hurt by the losses caused

31

by death. This may be someone in your own family—it could be your own self—or it may be a neighbor or someone not living in your community. Take some simple action to help that person, by writing the delayed note of condolence, baking a spice cake for the children of the bereaved family, or offering to sit with the aged widow who is alone so much of the time since her mate is dead. This is a particularly good discipline if you are fighting your own inner sorrow, since it will link you to others who face the same problem, showing you the universality of grief, and the elemental blessing of the promises of Easter's morning for daffodils.

Prayer: Dear Father, we pull away from grief and beg thee not to bring it into our lives, and yet it comes to each of us. Accept our thanks for thy promise to help us face loss, and to move with us into the days of the changing pattern. Help us to look ahead to the morning of daffodils when the time comes to leave our own little, established gardens for the glories of eternity. Amen.

5

Maytime and Memories

In front of the hospital entrance my husband and I sat wearily in our automobile that evening in May, thinking over the swift series of the day's events. Racing through our hearts was the jumble of facts concerning the emergency telephone call about the fall of an aged relative, impending surgery, accompanying legal details, and financial transactions.

All these were complicated by the fact that we lived a hundred miles from her home and the hospital. The throttle of trivia seemed to be stuck so that an endless exhaust was about to smother us in depression.

Along the street approaching the hospital came a middle-aged man, apparently walking home to his evening meal in a house nearby. He stopped at our car and slapped his hand against the hood.

"Nice car you have here," he said. "I sell a rival, but I sure do think this is a good car." Then he went swinging into the house, whistling as he shut the door.

Distracted by a thought different from the assortment of hospital problems, we glanced up to take a good look at our car. It was true, we did drive a fairly new car, and it was ready to take us on the freeways from work to the hospital and back again.

From this acknowledgment of blessings it was easy to go a step further and think how fortunate we were to be able to find good doctors, and a friendly hospital to take care of emergency patients. Silently we began to count these blessings, and the problem grew lighter.

Often I remember that salesman whistling on his way home in the May twilight, who made a simple, casual, cheerful remark to two strangers he was never to see again. Suppose he had made a disparaging remark about our car in our moment of gloom? Wouldn't this have triggered a great load of irritation and depression? Instead, his generous optimism changed our immediate thinking, resulting in large benefits.

Sometimes during the days of waiting at the hospital for improvement, we thought about him and wondered if this were a pattern of living with him, and somehow we thought that it might be his antidote for seeing the sad faces parked in front of his house night after night. What an inspiration he was to us, and an example for conduct.

For how often when we examine our memories do we find that a seemingly small incident has proved to be a larger one in changing our attitude and conduct for good or evil. The teacher who told us that we could learn to speak in public if we would make another effort saved us ultimately from perpetual stage fright. The man who showed the awkward boy how to operate a drill saw safely led him to hours of happy craftsmanship.

In the history books of our country there are countless incidents of soldiers on the field of battle in our own Civil War exchanging brotherly kindnesses. As a united nation we remember the gesture of Grant in allowing the southern soldiers to keep their horses as they would be needed in ploughing and planting for peace.

Probably nowhere is the simple gesture more appreciated than in our recollections of home and Mother whose special day is observed in May and which looms large in Maytime memories. We recall the flower on the tray taken into the sickroom, the special pudding made to tempt the appetite of the older aunt after surgery, and the soft touch of a hand on an arm in sympathy after the loss of a pet. These are things

35

which are woven into the fabric of a lifetime and serve to comfort not only at the original moment of sentimental impact, but over and over again in the following years, as they are remembered, perhaps after the giver has gone from this life.

Psychologists prove in their dealing with disturbed minds and hearts that it is often the smallest hurts that have festered and caused untold damage, long repressed. If the youngster can be persuaded to talk about what is hurting him, and bring it into his mind, perhaps the memory of the hurt can be taken away. Healing comes when he sees the slight in its true perspective—as a small thing which should not have bothered him. Yet we are so constituted that small things have enormous consequences. Therefore Maytime and memories should encourage us to make a new effort to see that our small actions are on the positive side, to help and not hurt.

Discipline for Inner Growth: Spend some time each day this month taking a clear look at your small actions during routine schedules. The longer you study them, the more they will appear to grow and not be small at all. At the end of the month you will have a growing awareness of the importance of watching the small actions—changing a defeatist word to a cheerful one, controlling a tendency to anger by refusing to speak the harsh word, and volunteering a word of hope when faced with a seemingly hopeless situation.

Discipline for Outer Action: Test the power of small acts to grow into great good by isolating some particular service you have wanted to do, but thought your own little bit would not help enough. This may mean sorting magazines in the family bookcase and taking the old ones to the nearest mental institution. It may mean stepping out doors and crossing the street to greet the new neighbor whose children at first seemed bothersome, and who are merely homesick. From the first action can come increased interest in prevention of mental disease which might strike in your own home. From the second can come a blessed neighborhood friendship. The point is to stir yourself out of the house and take the first small step on a route of friendliness to institutions or persons.

Prayer: Dear God, we have so much reason to be thankful to so many for the often-repeated small acts of kindness which have helped us on our way. Forgive us for the times when we have neglected to pass along this kindness to others nearest us. Help us to remember that in the eternal pattern there are no small actions, but all have great power to mold the human spirit closer to the image of God. Amen.

6

June Verse for the Month: "Blessed are the pure in heart: for they shall see God."—Matt. 5:8

Tissue and Veils

On the morning of her wedding day, an adored granddaughter received a precious word of advice from her beloved grandmother. "You think you are entering into a happy new world," said this wise older woman, "and it may very well be exactly that for you and your young man. But it's really not the world which will be different at all, unless the two of you make it different together."

She pointed out that marriage gave the young

38

woman an opportunity to try to make her part of the world what she wanted it to be deep in her own heart's desire. And she told her that when she herself had been married she had received this advice couched in different phrases. Her grandmother had said, "Make you the world a better place."

In this old colloquialism the accent had been on the "you" part of the sentence, placing responsibility squarely on the young bride to make herself into the kind of person who could be happy in the world which opened before her on her wedding day. The modern grandmother wisely sensed that today's brides, living in a machine age, sometimes have a tendency to overlook the necessity to develop as individuals and grow into places of responsibility in home and community.

Yet a better world is made of better individuals. With the problem of economic survival and the need for schools and churches, the pioneer women recognized the importance of living honorably as women, and offering strength individually to family and friends. They saw life realistically, with the tissue paper torn away from packages, and with veils pushed back from their faces as they began to cook on rusty, wood-burning stoves, and to start gardens from land reclaimed from the surrounding forest.

When trouble pushed in from all sides, the woman of the home knew that she had to make a little oasis of peace for herself. This she did in her rocking chair with a tatting shuttle in her hands. Today's grandmother and granddaughter may have to snatch a tiny moment of quiet while waiting for the red light to change to green at a traffic signal. But the need remains for a time of reflection on the direction of life.

For wearing a bridal veil and opening packages wrapped in tissue does not insure happy days ahead, as the mounting divorce statistics tell so graphically. Yet the beauty which surrounds even a simple wedding serves to focus attention on the fact that this is the beginning of a period when happiness can be heighened not only for the two individuals, but for those related in the family circle, and the friends in churches, clubs, and community.

Happiness must be shared, not only with each other but by opening the home to new friends if the man's employment takes him to another locality. The time comes when the bride must wrap in tissue a gift for another, newer bride. This gives opportunity to consider whether she has lived up to her ideals for marriage since the time of her own wedding showers.

Tissue, which seems so fragile, can prove surprisingly durable, as any honoree knows who has struggled with unwrapping a package while friends watched. Tissue is meant to be substantial enough to lend beauty to the object but to be cast aside when the time comes to make use of the gift itself.

Colorful wrappings which surround wedding gifts are designed to help provide beautiful memories. Some brides save all the ribbons from such packages, using them to stuff a satin boudoir pillow or for making an impromptu colorful bouquet of bows. Such trinkets help to remind the individual of the shower of good wishes, and enable her to bring into proper focus the dreams which are temporarily in shadow because of the discouragement of coping with realities of the budget or personality adjustments.

When the roast burns and the cake falls, it is hard to remember that these are not permanent disasters. What matters is the cheerful way in which the bride substitutes other dishes so the meal is not lost in gloom. It is not always possible to make the world into a better place, but it is always in order to try to "make you the world" a finer place. Certain disciplines help make the dreams of a happier world come true for those who desire it.

Discipline for Inner Growth: Walk to your china closet or bookcase and pick out the wedding or birthday gift which has meant the most to you. Think about why this is true. Is it because of the gift itself, or is it because of the memories it brings of the loving aunt, the college roommate who shared your fun, the employer who hated to have you leave but who understood your wish for a home or a new opportunity in travel? Reflect on the people behind the gifts, and what they have contributed to your personality.

41

Discipline for Outer Action: Concentrate in June on making yourself more nearly the type of person you visualized during your romantic courtship days or first job away from home. Did you want to be stronger and better able to face problems without flying to pieces? Then tackle the chore you have been putting off doing, whether it is making a budget or learning how to wash the living-room drapes. Did you want to make a place for your husband in the community? Then invite your pastor or the president of a service club in for dinner in your home, and forget the easy way of dining at a restaurant. Now is the time to put definite foundations under the dreams which accurately reflect your heart's desires for happiness.

Prayer: Father, we rejoice with all those who keep their dreams alive, and who move into marriage with high hopes for happiness. Comfort those who have felt their hearts break through disillusionment, and give them grace to begin again, firmly resolved to be happy now, wherever the tides of life may have deposited them. Let us grow through the happy and sad experiences of life so we may be fit for eternity with thee. Amen.

7

*July Verse for the Month: "And now,
Israel, what doth the Lord thy God require of thee,
but to fear the Lord thy God, to walk in all his ways,
and to love him, and to serve the Lord
thy God with all thy heart and with
all thy soul."—Deut. 10:12*

A Little Walk Together

When I was a little girl my favorite walk
took me past a big yard with a white picket fence.
As soon as I knew how to count, I practiced my num-
bers by letting my fingers lightly touch the top of each
fence post as I walked to the store on errands for my
mother.

There were houses to count, and kittens and pup-
pies in certain yards. Near the corner was the church

43

with its steeple, and over on the opposite corner was the store itself with a wide assortment of boxes and packages from which to choose good things to eat.

Sometimes a playmate would go on the walk with me, or a visiting adult, or a new neighbor. Then there were other things to point out of special interest which I sometimes took for granted when walking alone.

One morning on such a walk my grandfather told me of how his own grandfather had walked westward from his home on the eastern shores, coming by foot to build a new home in the midwest and establish his own family. Then I learned that this was the way America had been formed, as pioneers walked from one fertile spot to another, in search of a place to build homes, schools, and churches.

With limited funds for amusements, walking together had been a favorite enjoyment in these early days as whole families went out to a certain picnic spot near the river's edge. Sometimes, through the ritual of walking together to pick the purple wild flowers or to gather the crimson leaves of autumn, friendships were formed which lasted for years.

Walking races provided amusement at the group picnics formed to celebrate July Fourth, the birthday anniversary of America. In fact, the forming of our government had been in itself a means of citizens taking a little walk together, marching abreast in unison toward goals of freedom for all.

Each individual was to have the right to walk in the path of his own choice, to select his vocation in line with his own talents, to decide how he wanted to earn his living. He was to be free to walk to the church of his own faith, and to go inside to worship God in freedom of conscience. All children of whatever race, color, or creed were to be free to attend school, for opportunities were to be provided for all to gain an education.

The personal touch remained in a world where people walked together to the town meetinghouse to discuss plans of interest to their mutual welfare.

As the mechanized age came along, some of this individual interest and initiative was removed. Walking almost became a lost art, and with it went some of the personal interest in problems which could sometimes be solved as people walked together toward a common meeting place. Problems literally flew in on the wings of airplanes which could circle the globe in short time, bringing word of wars in far places which involved the boy down on the corner.

The need became urgent to keep alive the spirit of walking together. For nobody knows how far the trail leads from a little walk together in understanding. Sometimes I have asked myself two questions: What is time itself but the opportunity to walk for a little while the paths of earth? What is life itself but a succession of little walks together?

If this be true, then the manner of our daily

45

walk together becomes of utmost importance. Surely there is a lesson in the excitement on the face of a baby who first takes a step alone. Perhaps nothing else in life will ever bring the same look of joy in achievement. Instead, it is this first upright step which is one of the things which distinguishes man from other members of the animal kingdom.

The opportunity for a little walk together remains one of man's greatest blessings in a world of confusion and turmoil. There is a secret talisman for peace and serenity in the continued remembrance of the power of fellowship generated in a little walk together.

In July, when the birthday of America is marked, there are certain disciplines involving walking which can lead to a better display of citizenship and use of its privileges.

Discipline for Inner Growth: Take a walk by yourself on some road which you usually do not frequent. This may mean first driving to a spot away from home in your car. It may be just walking home from the grocery store since you may not have walked the block since moving to the new neighborhood. Get the perspective of walking in an area usually seen from a moving vehicle. And have the joy of doing this alone, giving you a chance to catch up on your own thoughts. Walking is a clue to creativity, whether planning family meals, painting a picture, or designing a dress.

Discipline for Outer Action: Walk inside some community institution you have never visited. If you have never been on jury duty, step inside the town courtroom and see the American flag flying in a room where twelve men and women listen to evidence and consider the guilt or innocence of a person charged with some crime. Or walk inside a modern church and survey the new plastic windows, meditating on how the same light filters through all. Walk to the benefit sale of a minority church group, linking yourself to America's heritage of many nationalities, each contributing a food specialty and typical music to our enjoyment.

Prayer: Father, we are grateful that we may have thee as a companion on our daily walks through life. Forgive us for allowing monotony to obscure the joy of a little walk together. Give us feet eager to do thy errands, whatever the path they lead us to explore in thy name. Amen.

47

8

The Gift of a Mountain

When my neighbor knocked at the door that hot summer afternoon she said, "Come outside with me. I want to give you back your mountain."

So we went together to the edge of the porch near the chairs in which we sit to watch the sunset, and it was true that the mountain had come back to dominate our beautiful view. My neighbor had made this generous gift by thoughtfully trimming the bushy branches from a tree on her side of the street which

48

had grown unruly and sufficiently high to block the view of the wonderful mountain in the nearby vacation area.

"I didn't know until the other night that you could no longer enjoy the view," she told me simply. "I don't want to be guilty of keeping anyone from seeing that mountain."

Together we stood to look at its serene strength as the mountain guards our little town, with the groves of orange trees, steeples of churches, roofs of hospitals and schools. The tall peak seems to smile kindly on the newcomers who live in the houses of subdivisions, houses whose pink, blue, and yellow paint makes them look like modernistic flowers attached to cement stems as sidewalks lead to roads.

In good weather and bad, the mountain looks down on the activities of merchants heading to unlock their stores, doctors en route to homes of shut-ins, and mothers hanging up socks and shirts of their children. We like seeing it silhouetted at sunrise when we go out to the garden for the morning paper, which brings news of the world from afar to the mountain and its valley.

It seemed so large we did not think anything could take it from our view. But the quick-growing variety of tree across the street shot upward at such an angle that even the tall mountain began to seem smaller. Why didn't we tell our neighbor about it? Because she had a right to her tree, and we did not want to

49

risk hurting her feelings or pressing our own wishes too firmly.

But we felt a sense of loss as the mountain shrank from sight. Then one evening, looking up from our porch, our neighbor had seen what the tree was doing, and had ordered it trimmed for our better view. Nobody ever gave us a nicer vacation present, for we can stay home and enjoy the ever-changing panorama as the sun moves across the sky with shadows on the hilltop.

Our neighbor sits with us to enjoy the beauty. Sometimes we talk about how a simple action restored a wonderful view, and increased our understanding of each other. We remember how little details often keep us from full appreciation of great blessings, and that this is especially true in travel. Whining and complaining about the heat or the mosquitoes can ruin the day's fishing trip for the man of the house, who needed the vacation from a tense desk job.

Chronic bickering among the children in the backseat of the car can make the mother wish she had stayed home and not attempted to visit the aging relative. Stinginess over money matters in paying a restaurant check can spoil the relationship among friends of many years' standing. All these are the little "underbrush" which blocks the view.

While it is sad when it happens on a weekend vacation trip close to home, it can be of greater tragic import when tourists are traveling in another country. Comparing the abundance available at home can make someone in a host country wish that the American had stayed at his own smug desk in the first place. The image of our whole country can be changed by the selfishness of a tourist ordering others around because he knows they are dependent upon his tips for moving bags onto busses or cleaning a room in a hillside inn.

Yet great good can come from sharing a view together, once the underbrush which chokes the view is cut away with one understanding act. The simplest way to start is with a smile which wipes away frowns, and sometimes serves as language in a port far from home. Friendliness is an attitude which bridges boundaries, whether in making life more pleasant for your neighbor who shares hot summer days with you, or the person you meet on far distant shores on a long-awaited summer trip.

Each of us can have the joy of giving the beauty of a fresh view to ourselves and others by adopting friendly attitudes.

Discipline for Inner Growth: Try to become aware of what your own area offers in the way of vacation beauty. If you have lived in the area for a long time, pretend that you are a newcomer. If you are newly arrived, ask a neighbor to help you make a list of nearby attractions. Is there a stained-glass window in your church with an interesting history? When you find out, spend some time indoors away from summer sun, reflecting on the window's meaning. Is there a monument to pioneers at a stream nearby? Rest beside it. Make a list of at least six possible places to explore with friends.

Discipline for Outer Action: In order to change your own viewpoint and see life from some-one else's front porch, make a real effort this vacation to find out "how the other half lives." If you must economize on a rigid budget most of the year, treat yourself to a good luncheon at a nearby resort to avoid that expensive attitude of self-pity. If you have grown flabby from too much pampering of palate, eat at a nearby small counter which caters to transients. Share your substance by furnishing refreshments for a vacation church school in a minority-group area in your community. Or make a gift of time by chaperoning a picnic or swimming party.

Prayer: God of beauty in the vast out-of-doors, forgive us for binding our own hearts so that we cannot fathom the abundance closest to us. Keep us from hindering the view of any of our neighbors by our blindness to our faults of unfriendliness. Help us to have carefree vacation hearts throughout the year by keeping our attitudes unfettered and our eyes open to oppportunities for good. Amen.

9

September Verse for the Month: *"And thou,*
Solomon, my son, know thou the God of thy father, and
serve him with a perfect heart and with
a willing mind."—I Chr. 28:9

So I Can Read to Me

With her arms filled with tiny books, the
five-year-old came into the room where I sat with
my mending. She spilled the bright covers onto the
floor and plunked herself down beside them. Her
plaid skirt billowed out over the green carpet like a
balloon coming to rest in a meadow.

"Look at them," she said, nodding her curls so
vigorously that the red ribbon bounced. At first I

thought she meant she wanted me to read aloud to her. But her face was unhappy and her voice almost angry as with one chubby hand she pounded the cover of a book, in contrast to her usual gentle handling of her favorite toys.

So I put the mending to one side and asked if there was something I could do to help. She came closer and put a trusting hand into mine and said, "Please, will you get me a book that I can read to me?"

She had sensed what joy adults had in reading to themselves as well as reading aloud her own story-books, and she wanted my help in securing a book which she could read for herself. Soon now she would acquire reading skill, and then there would be no end to the books she could read for herself.

Looking at her earnest face, I was reminded anew of the great blessing of being able to read to myself. In how many lonely moments at home, in a hospital, in happy travel, has the joy of reading proved a blessing.

Automatically my hand went to the copy of the Bible on the reading table beside the mending basket. Solemnly I made a special promise to my small friend. "When you learn how to read we will get for you a copy of the best book of all for *'I to read to me.'*"

She smiled happily and relaxed on the floor with her favorite picture books, obviously anticipating the day when she could read sentences, paragraphs, and pages. I thought how her interest in books had been started when her young mother put transparent tape over the edges of the covers to safely enclose the pages, turning the tiny books into baby blocks which the child could fondle.

Then grandparents had read aloud to her when she could hardly distinguish the sound of words from the song of a lullaby. Small wonder that she knew the joys of reading. Ready now to accept books, her character might be determined in large part by what kind of books fell into her hands as she moved from early childhood into adolescence and on to an adulthood.

Even as I thought of the possibilities opening wide for her, I wondered why many lose the thrill of reading. Is it because of the increasing encroachment on time by television, radio, or out-of-door sports? Or is it because in a speeded-up world we tend to accept summaries and condensations of great works, rather than to read the complete versions for ourselves.

Perhaps it is because as individuals we fail to map out a plan of reading in any specific field of interest. No matter what that subject may be, there are many books to encourage a native interest, whether in cake baking, repairing automobiles, flower arrangement, or sewing for a family. Aside from these practical subjects, there are books covering the range of imaginative poetry, the history of America, and the detailed study of flowers and birds of any given area.

The happiest readers are those who decide what is of most interest "so I can read to me" happily, pursuing some definite trend leading to intellectual and emotional development. Once this course of study is decided upon, the way usually opens to find time to continue the reading, even if it has to be sandwiched in between household tasks.

Late at night proves a particularly good time to read books in the field of religion, for tests indicate that the last thoughts which control the mind before dropping off to sleep seem to have a lasting value through the hours of rest. Sometimes the subconscious works on the material, so that if stories of courage have been read the individual has more of this virtue in meeting the next day's tasks. The cumulative effect of such a habit leads to decisiveness. In September, when school bells ring for the start of new courses, there are certain steps which can help to educate hearts of all ages.

Discipline for Inner Growth: Enroll in the school of right living by taking a refresher course in your own Bible. Use your concordance to look up such words as "faith," "hope," "love," picking out the words which you most need to use in your own daily activities. Then look up the total Bible passage surrounding the key word as listed in your concordance. Follow through with all the pertinent verses in the Old and New Testaments before moving on to a different word, important in managing your life. This

57

activity will increase your spiritual vocabulary and give verses to help when troubled.

Discipline for Outer Action: Now is the right moment to do something for those who lack your own advantages in the way of owning books and magazines. Surely there is at least one magazine you can share with a settlement-house library, or a book you can pack for mailing to a missionary. Perhaps your church needs a library, and a committee could be formed to go about collecting books from individual homes. Maybe it is your own community library which needs a fresh approach to the recruiting of books. Have the joy of sending a cash donation to the nearest Braille Institute, which serves the blind with talking books and literature transcribed into dots read by sensitive fingers.

Prayer: God, we are grateful for the words of life, and we need help in translating them into modern living. Teach us to put the Bible truths into positive action that we may know the abundant life of which the Scripture speaks. As we help others with their own problems, may they find us individuals with truly educated hearts. Amen.

10

Try Giving It Away First

When I told a gracious older friend how very much I longed for a certain new possession, she said to me kindly, "Then you must give something away first."

She explained that a part of her philosophy of living was that she must make room for the coming of the new gift, whether material or spiritual. "Don't be afraid to give away the old to make room for the new."

59

Why are we so reluctant to give things away first? Because of this gnawing fear that they may not be replaced. Yet the getting ready for new things may be an important part of their fulfillment. This is important to remember when October comes and club and church groups resume their quick tempo after a summer lull. Civic projects take new emphasis, and often there are financial drives for community-wide benefit.

Is it sometimes hard for you to find your way through the maze of activities? Then the advice to "give it away first" can make for successful living. Do you want to take up a new activity? Then gracefully let go of the old one, and allow life to bring the new interest to your side.

This is extremely difficult when a person has encountered sorrow within the year, and wants to cling to old remembered patterns and yet misses the familiar companions taken by death who formerly shared the joys of the group. Give away your interest by encouraging some newcomer to enter, and through that person may come a new line of thought for your own discouraged heart.

Maybe the problem is too many activities, so that none of them are enjoyed. A professor friend of mine is constantly going through her bookcase to find a book to give to a student. "I can't stand a jammed-up bookcase," she told me once. "Books have to have room to breathe." This is also true of happy living, for

60

too many activities crammed too close together leave none of them time to breathe in the pure air of companionship. Give up one of the activities and enjoy the more those which remain.

Hardest of all to give away first are the old resentments and bitterness, the feuds with those with whom we have had disagreements. Perhaps by long association these negative qualities have become our "friends," and that old enemy—fear—keeps us from letting them go. If we surrender them, there may even be room for friendship on a beginning basis with the one previously disliked. It is often true that the strong reaction against a person is part of the inherent pull of opposites which could lead to a great enjoyment of personalities.

Sometimes even our friendships have to be given away first before growth comes. Even with the best of intentions to remain on the same basis, we sometimes outgrow the past and its pleasant associations. New circumstances keep our time pattern from being that of our former associates. Perhaps they move away, and we feel sorry for ourselves that the pleasant pattern has been disturbed.

Then we need to release these friends into the keeping of God and look around for those close to us who are longing for new friendships themselves. Is it the woman who has moved into your block? Or the man who has come to work in the store next door? Perhaps it is a foreign student who attends your church spasmodically?

Memories of the church back home can so fill the mind that the heart fails to see the need for workers in the new church on the corner, built where the orange grove formerly stood. Hardest of all to give away first are precious memories. Yet when they are given to the past, there is a chance for the present to flood in with its realities, which can create a happy tomorrow.

With fall's activities recruiting new members there is opportunity to become integrated in the new location, or to find a zestful, fresh point of view in the old situation. Life is kept fluid by the process of giving away first the extra possessions and old attitudes.

One way to keep the channels of living open so that more can come to be enjoyed and used is to learn to practice with mere material things the needed spiritual art involved in the process of "giving it away first." Here are practical suggestions to put into use as October brings new activity into your area.

Discipline for Inner Growth: In a quiet time list honestly the things you would find it hardest to give away—dishes, clothes, furniture, records, books. Then force yourself to reflect on the obvious fact that truly someday all which you now own will belong to someone who survives you. This is never an easy fact to face, but ultimately all possessions of material nature are left behind. Once this is realized, it is easier to resolve to be happy in this lifetime by sharing with others and learning the joy of giving.

Discipline for Outer Action: Open the door of your clothes closet and study its contents. No matter how limited your wardrobe is, there is surely at least one garment which you can share with someone else. Take the coat or suit or dress or blouse from the hook and deliver it personally to the community project of your choice. While there find out more about how this is operated, whether a P.T.A. closet for young people, a mission packing operation for orphans in the Orient, or a city-wide thrift store where others may buy at small charge. Those who regularly each fall practice this exercise declare that this sorting of their wardrobes with a view to what may be given away to others gives them a fresh perspective and enjoyment of the clothes remaining. Often they themselves feel better dressed even without a new garment.

Prayer: God who clothes this world with beauty, we thank thee for caring for our own physical needs. Forgive us for our failure to enjoy life at

63

its maximum best because of our fearful holding on to possessions which should be shared. May we be persons of faith who can first give it away, trusting thee to fill our lives with the most of what is best for our own hearts. Amen.

11

With Thankful Hands

When I opened the envelope, out fell a piece of white drawing paper. On it were traced five hands, one inside the other, the largest one on the outside and the others lined up within this happy boundary.

The only words were written at the bottom of the sheet. Printed in bright red crayon was the phrase, "All our family thanks you for your gift."

As I held the paper in my hand I could almost see

65

what had happened in this home to which our package had gone. The outer, larger hand obviously belonged to the busy father of the family. Mother had persuaded him to put his hand on the blank paper while someone had traced around it with a blue pencil. Perhaps this had been the five-year-old son who adores his Dad.

Maybe the young mother had put her own gentle hand over his to hold it steady, before she in turn placed her hand inside the drawing of his larger one to have her fingers traced on the sheet.

Then the son came next with his chubby fist just right to hold a baseball. Daughter had put aside her doll long enough to let her dainty hand be traced. This fat little hand in the center could belong to nobody but the adorable baby. How had she kept still long enough for the tracing, I wondered!

Yet there were five hands, all outstretched in gratitude for the simple gift from our home to theirs. This "thank-you" project somehow brought to me in heartwarming fashion all their own happiness in building a home together. For they had chosen as their thank-you symbol, the traced hands of a family working as a unit. They had included the paw print of their beloved cat, "Smokey."

Looking at this precious note, I thought of the families where the mother has all the thank-you notes to write. There are other homes where much fussing and confusion ensues when attempts are made to get the children to write the necessary thank-yous to aunts and uncles for birthday gifts.

Sometimes there are lonely hearts in the homes of grandparents because the thank-you note never is written. Yet it takes just a minute to pause in gratitude and say "thank you" by tracing the hands of the family. There are other ways in which hands may be lifted in gratitude.

One of the best ways is to offer them up in prayer to God for his blessings, by saying grace at the table. There is strength for the day in the outstretched hands of the members of all ages, reaching out to clasp hands in the circle of the family. By pausing to thank God for food, and for strength for the tasks of the day, there is generated more strength to meet the extra demands which the day may present.

Thankful hands get to work for others by joining in group projects within the community to make it a better place for others. In this there are many modern counterparts of the pioneer's sharing of talents in the joining together to build a house or a barn. The sociability inherent in such work projects leads now to projects which are aimed at discouraging juvenile delinquency.

Young people find their own skills developed and their understanding of the needs of others magnified as they work at building bookcases for a settlement house or painting dormitories at a mission school.

Work with the hands emphasizes the spiritual truths of sharing which they have been discussing in church Sunday classes.

The ability to say thank-you with our hands is one which remains with us to the end of a life-span in usual cases. Often older members of the church can make their special contribution by furnishing handwork which they have made through the year for a church bazaar. It may be colorful pot holders, or stationery decorated with tatted flowers or hand-painted nosegays, but the work of the hands expresses gratitude of the heart. November is a good month to think of daily blessings of hand and heart, and to develop them through the exercise of definite disciplines.

Discipline for Inner Growth: Take yourself from the center of your world by thinking of all the hands which minister to you and your family. Start with your kitchen cupboard and make a list of people involved in bringing the breakfast food to your kitchen—truck driver, package designer, maker of colored inks, grower of the grain, irrigator of the field. Use this as a simple exercise to become aware of the hands which feed your family. Move from the kitchen to the living room and on to the garden to stretch your concept of your reliance on other hands.

Discipline for Outer Action: Literally use your hands, whether in molding a loaf of old-fashioned homemade bread, digging in the soil, smoothing the brow of a sick child, or playing the neglected piano or organ. If you are particularly nervous, go down town during this period and secure a piece of needlepoint, cross-stitch, or knitting, and get all the necessary instructions to complete a chair seat, tablecloth, or sweater. Learn the rhythm of working with your hands, and what this does to stimulate your heart and mind into constructive, peaceful channels.

Prayer: Father, whose eternal hands formed the world and all that is therein, we thank thee for fashioning us in thine own loving image. We acknowledge our dependence upon thy hands of good, and those of all our known and unknown brothers on earth. Help us to use our hands for thee, reflecting in their actions our gratitude for life, and our loving concern for our neighbors. Amen.

12

December Verse for the Month: "For God
so loved the world, that he gave his only begotten Son,
that whosoever believeth in him should not perish,
but have everlasting life."—John 3:16

Rich Gifts Without Money

"Our family always had such fun choosing Christmas gifts," sighed the woman near me at the department-store counter, "but with high taxes and inflated prices it isn't as much fun as it used to be. I guess what I really need is a substitute for money."

She did not know it, perhaps, but she always has in her possession a substitute for money at any gift-buying time. That is found in the warmhearted wish to share time, talent, and possessions. Anyone can learn how this is accomplished and have the joy of making rich gifts without money being involved.

Start with what you already possess, perhaps the morning newspaper or a monthly magazine. Clip recipes from the advertising section or homemaking pages, and mount them on 3x5 cards or pieces of cardboard. This is one of my most cherished shower gifts, made by an elderly friend with the assistance of small children of the neighborhood she had gathered in to help on a rainy afternoon.

Take a good look around your own room or rented quarters, or the old family home in which you live. There, you did find a duplicate of something, didn't you? Perhaps it was just an extra pencil in your desk drawer, but the child down the street would enjoy seeing it tucked in his Christmas stocking so he can draw pictures of space rockets.

Perhaps your cupboards have been emptied in moving to another part of the country, or the items sold to meet financial burdens caused by long illness or death of a loved one. Then use your skill of hand and brain. One of the most beloved older couples in a community are the two people who make it a habit to teach the children in the block a new skill on each birthday. One little girl is counting the days until she is nine years old because on that day she is to be taught a new knitting stitch.

Consider the surplus of what may be ordinary to

you and which may prove a real delicacy to your friends. Take an inventory of the glasses of fig jam you made last summer when your tree was overflowing with fruit, and see if you do not have some glasses to share with others. Is there a tree of wild nuts you pass on your morning walk? Or what about the shells from your nearest beach, or rocks from the desert?

Use available free sources of information by taking a few minutes to write to travel agencies and secure bright folders for the young couple who need to keep alive their dreams of travel despite current financial setbacks. To the bedfast veteran such folders can prove of real therapeutic value in changing the mind's monotony, as hospital workers testify.

Seek out your own souvenirs of travel tucked away in some bookcase. Remember that even the loan of a painting at the right time can constitute a welcome gift as it brightens up temporary living quarters. Even your last, sample ballot can become a real gift by helping new American citizens learn English in their settlement-house naturalization classes.

You may decide you have nothing of tangible nature left to divide with others. There is still your own handwriting with which to copy down on a tablet the lines of a poem or quotation which blessed your own marriage. Its philosophy might ultimately do more for the young newlyweds than more elaborate gifts of silver.

Devise a simple, standard, trademark gift of your own. One woman makes brightly colored felt holders for needles and pins in the shape of tiny sunbonnet girls whose lace nosegays conceal places for holding the necessary mending equipment. Another makes hot-dish holders shaped like the fresh fruits which grow in her locality, changing the design and shape each season for variety.

Let your financial gifts serve double duty. When you are able to make any contribution to church or club bazaar, let your funds be spent wisely as gifts for others, and keep them stored in a special gift box. There is usually a table of inexpensive gifts—crocheted bookmarks, handpainted place cards, ceramic buttons. By choosing these as selections for your slender money contributions you may help the cause you select and still build a reserve of gifts. Particularly is this a double or triple blessing if the gifts have been made by shut-ins who receive a percentage of the income from the bazaar table.

Christmas is a good time to take a look at your materialistic attitudes which may be spoiling your year-round fun in giving. Here are ways to increase your pleasure and enlarge your heart.

Discipline for Inner Growth: Take your gift list of things to buy and analyze why you have put down a fishing tackle or book on furniture repair or a silver necklace. Find out in your own mind the reason back of your wish to give this item. Is it to

73

show the ability to spend generously, or is it really because this expresses what the friend or relative most firmly wants and needs for personal enjoyment? Satisfy yourself that you are thinking in terms of the recipient's wishes and not gratifying your own selfish pride in giving. If the latter, substitute a less expensive gift more in line with the recognized desires of the recipient.

Discipline for Outer Action: Reverse your usual plan of giving, which in most homes involves expensive gifts to those who have much and less expensive to those who have little. Give yourself the fun of ferreting out a most inexpensive gift for your wealthiest relative or friend. You may find you please him mightily by presenting him with a bag of pine cones in a red mesh sack, something for a fragrant Christmas fire which will warm his heart because of your remembrance of his love of the out-of-doors. Make your substantial gift of medicine or an electric blanket quietly, anonymously if possible, to someone who lives modestly and gives all year, perhaps in a professional job which is poorly paid.

Prayer: God, it is hard for us to learn how to give. It is even harder for us to learn how to receive from others, and how to accept that greatest of all gifts which came to the world at the first Christmastime. Help us to live as thy children, growing steadily as we learn how to give of ourselves to others in thy name. Amen.

Disciplines
to Help You Solve
Specific Problems

13

*Verse for Livelines: "See, I have
set before thee this day life and good, and death
and evil."—Deut. 30:15*

Deadlines or Livelines

"When I stopped working in an office to
stay home I thought I was all finished with deadlines,"
said my young friend as she surveyed her littered sewing room, stacks of unread magazines, correspondence
to be answered, and a file of recipes to be tried out
"someday." She felt defeated by all the trivia which
continued to accumulate without any definite decision of action.

"It doesn't seem right to think of deadlines in con-

79

nection with a home," she told me. Yet it was obvious she needed some system to get things done. Together we coined a word to fit our own situations—"liveline" with the accent on living.

These livelines have added zest to daily living, and enabled those who use them to accomplish more than formerly. Anybody can establish workable livelines by taking the positive attitude toward deadlines.

Both words imply that there is a certain time limit at which a designated piece of work must be finished, before moving to the next exciting project. In the career woman's life if the required article is not written by the deadline, then the editor must put another piece into the magazine. Next time he deals with another writer.

Because there is no one to impose such realistic substitution within the home, the housewife falls into the habit of thinking she does not need to meet a time schedule. Yet in many ways she and her family fail to achieve happiness because of this, and face punishments just as rigorous as for those who fail to meet business deadlines.

What housewife really likes a littered sewing room, with half-finished garments piled on top of the cedar chest, or patterns dropping to the floor and getting mixed in with others? All this clutter can be avoided by a self-imposed liveline which says, "Do not begin the new dress until the current one is completed."

Are the Christmas letters still unanswered when

summer comes? Then agree that they must be finished by July Fourth, or they must go into the wastebasket and be carried outside with the trash. Just such a drastic liveline may be needed to persuade your better self to write fresh letters at next holiday season.

Setting aside fifteen minutes at the end of the week to sort out the magazines can keep your library rack from becoming so involved that you decide to stop subscribing to magazines you never get around to reading. If the discards are given away promptly to others in the neighborhood or to your church library, they have double value than when they are saved until outdated. A liveline can keep your family more fully informed about what is going on in this interesting world.

This system can save much fatigue, for psychologists say that there is almost nothing more tiring than the feeling of being "pushed" and having many things to do, none of which are being accomplished. The modern-day equivalent of the old bundle of sticks must be broken down into small pieces, each of which can be easily carried to its destination. The entire bundle may be dropped and scattered aimlessly over a wide area, leading to endless frustration in picking up the important pieces to begin over again.

The next time you fall behind schedule at home, and have that hopeless feeling of fatigue and distress which comes from seeing things you want to do and never seem to find time for, think about setting up

81

your own system of livelines for your home. It will help to take the sameness out of housework, for each home can plan livelines for the accomplishment of pet projects.

When one project is behind you, there will be zest and joy in moving ahead to something new. The mind is clearer with the first task out of the way, and there is strength gained in just the act of finishing an item. This seems to act as a stimulant, giving a running start for the next activity. You will want to get ready to live more fully by finishing one task and turning to another, since you are in charge of your own livelines. At first you may need to move slowly in setting up such a system, and here are some simple disciplines to help put the plan in action.

Discipline for Inner Growth: This is a nasty exercise which at first you will not like, but which leads to later happiness. First you must be honest with yourself and pick out the task you most dislike to do. Are you the world's worst ironer of blouses? Then you must take a blouse out of your closet, wash it and iron it to begin this exercise. If it doesn't look right when you are finished, do it over again, and then go on to the next blouse. If you despise writing letters, pick out the one which has been longest unanswered and write a brief note to that correspondent to start reducing the pile. Do the worst task first, and the rest become easier.

Discipline for Outer Action: Forget yourself, and look around your family circle, or your group of friends, or your club. Think in terms of what these people might like to do, and have long put off doing because a time limit has not been set. Have you promised each other that you would go see the nearby public gardens? Then go this month, for surely something will be in flower, even if not your favorite spring daffodils or fall chrysanthemums. Go now, in the month when you are practicing this exercise, and you will have learned how to get to the garden, the admission price, and how best to enjoy it on repeated visits. Help generate pleasure for others by keeping to your own scheduled liveline for happiness.

Prayer: Father of the universe, we covet some small knowledge of thy laws of action which brought into being the world which is our home. Help us to live in it more happily by keeping abreast of the activities of the changing days. Forgive us for using delaying tactics which cripple the joy of living, and give us free hearts. Amen.

14

Verse for Avoiding Damage: "Now I rejoice, not that ye were made sorry, but that ye sorrowed to repentance: for ye were made sorry after a godly manner, that ye might receive damage by us in nothing."—II Cor. 7:9

Damage Through Carelessness

Because he wanted a music cabinet of great beauty, the home owner selected pieces of wood which would match in grain and texture when placed together.

If the grain of a fresh piece appeared different from the previous piece selected, it was instantly discarded. No small blemish was to be allowed to spoil the completed cabinet.

84

He employed an expert workman to assemble the pieces with great care so that this piece of furniture would command much admiration when finished and on display in the living room.

When the carpenter had finished his work, the cabinet was brought to the home to see if it would fit in the corner planned for it, and the dimensions and design were declared ideal. Eagerly the family looked forward to having this stained a color to match the table and organ.

Meanwhile painters were engaged with instructions to "paint the living room tan." Seeing the cabinet pushed up against the wall they were to paint, they surveyed its unfinished exterior and decided it must be a part of the new woodwork of the room.

One of the newly engaged members of the crew walked across to the cabinet and with a few quick strokes covered the matched grained wood with the tan wall paint. In these few seconds the effect of the pattern of the expensive wood was entirely destroyed through the splashing on of inexpensive paint.

All the time and money of the owner in planning for his beautiful cabinet had been wasted in this one quick mistake. Now no one could see in the furniture the natural beauty of the wood from God's forest, adapted to the melodies of music within the home.

This costly mistake happened because the home owner neglected one simple detail. He forgot to tell the painters that he wanted his unpainted cabinet left undisturbed, awaiting a special finish.

It is often the one neglected detail which causes sorrow in personal life, tragedy in the development of personality or character, or loss of a business reputation or personal income.

Certainly in the building of a useful life, care should be taken to see that in one single stroke of surrender to temptation or discouragement, the building which has been a lifetime in the making is not lost.

Splashy paints of indulgence can so easily cover the fine pattern of character which has been long in the making. As in the case of the cabinet it is time consuming to try to remove the surface evidences of the mistake, and the newness never returns to the same degree.

Fortunately for the individual who makes one damaging stroke of error there is always opportunity to try again through repentance and an honest endeavor to rebuild the cabinets of life. But the ruined piece of wood lost to beauty by quick carelessness reminds us of the wisdom of trying to avoid making the damaging mistake in the first place.

This calls for taking a good look at the items which cause such losses. Is the trouble founded on a quick temper which alienates those who wish to help? Is it based on sharp speech which wounds the feelings of those whose cooperation is needed to finish the project?

Perhaps the damaging stroke lies in a too hurried attitude which overlooks the need for patience in bringing to a successful ending the great dreams of the beginning. Maybe the individual trusts too completely the attitudes of others who do not fully comprehend the significance of the matter.

Thoughtless acceptance of shortcuts or unwillingness to count the cost in time and energy can ruin the project. To avoid such personal disasters, certain disciplines can be put into practice which bring perfection and harmony as closer realities.

Discipline for Inner Growth: List your five most recent failures, whether a cake which fell and could not be iced, or an embarrassing incident in a club meeting, or an inability to cope with a problem brought to you by a child. Consider carefully what you feel caused the failure, and then see if the five are not in some way linked together, no matter how separate they seem on the surface. A cake can fall from being taken from the oven too soon, misunderstanding with a fellow club officer can arise through haste, and a child's problem be ignored because "mother hasn't time just now." When you have found the identifying factor recurring over and over in your failures, you can correct it and be on the way to future success.

Discipline for Outer Action: Go directly to the area where you fail most often, and determine to make a success of one simple project in this field. This is important because it will result in a growth of confidence which spreads to other areas. Did you stumble and stammer the last time you tried to announce the women's circle program? Is it impossible for you to pray in public? These first defeats need not be damaging experiences. You are not a block of wood, but a human being, and so can try again. If the remarks of others have frightened you, these can be removed by keeping the mind fixed on God for help. You have power in your heart to refuse to let a damaging stroke come from any outside source.

Prayer: Father, it is hard for us to keep from failing, particularly when life moves so fast around us. Sometimes it seems that one failure leads on to another, and damaging stroke piles on top of damaging stroke. Keep us from making that first stroke or permitting an outside stroke to permanently damage our hearts. Amen.

15

Verse for the Heart's Companion:
"I am a companion of all them that fear thee, and
of them that keep thy precepts."—Ps. 119:63

The Heart's Companion

Explorers who have returned from India tell of the importance of having a tame elephant to lead the wild elephants captured in jungle hunts. Without the aid of the elephant which has been made gentle by its tamers, it would be impossible for men to subdue the strong beasts when they are first captured.

Elephant hunts call for the building of a huge, wooden stockade carefully covered as a lair. Into this the elephants are herded by burning brush fires strategically placed behind them.

When the elephants find they have been trapped, they use all their strength to try to push down the stockade. But it is so made that pushing will only tighten the web of wooden posts. Eventually the animals stop their pushing, and turn to fighting among themselves. Only when they are hungry and weakened do they seek a way out.

Even then they would not willingly follow their captors without the help of the elephants who have learned the ways of civilization. The mahouts who ride on top of the elephants carefully chain one tamed elephant to a wild one, and thus the new arrival from the jungle comes out into the clearing where there is food and water for him.

A little later the tame elephant shackled to the wild one takes him down to the river to swim and bathe. Eventually the animal accepts the daily routine in captivity and seems to anticipate the daily jaunt to the river and the feeding bins. Thus he is able to carry the burdens, to be of help in building roads and cities.

In this gentling process there is an example for those who increasingly face problems of trying to aid others involved in jungles of confusion. Sometimes young people become so involved in delinquency that there seems no way for them to break loose from wild habits and be tamed to the laws and demands of adult citizenship. Then the help of a stronger companion can be of great blessing and benefit to the young person, his family, and the community which needs the use of his talent when educated and put to good use.

Whether the violent conduct is caused by current sinning or remorse over past failures, there are always hurt hearts which need to be made gentle in order to live effectively in the future. Sometimes such individuals rebel against early efforts to help them, even as the animals thrash about in their compound. It is then that the need is greatest for one who already has come through an experience of sorrow or loss to try to lead the one who needs help into new pathways of service.

If one elephant is helped by another, how much more true is it that a human heart may be helped by a friend. All of us at one time or another in a lifetime have need for the fellowship of a heart's companion. Indeed, the road in pleasant weather can be made more enjoyable by being yoked with a strong companion who understands the need of the heart.

This principle of action not only helps where disturbed individuals are concerned, but is useful in building a happy marriage and developing wholesome children able to cope with the demands of the space age. The presence of a stronger companion can keep the child from going off into paths which are dangerous, and is a technique which is useful in avoiding unpleasant consequences.

91

If, however, the situation already is complicated through neurosis or mental illness, great healing power for good can be found in the simple process of adopting a heart's companion. A part of therapy for the mentally disturbed involves having volunteer workers who will sit near the patients, ready to listen if they wish to speak. One such worker said the greatest thrill of her days of volunteer service came when after long silence such a person said "hello," as a first step back to clear thinking.

All of us can learn to be the heart's companion for others, if we will think about developing strong traits which will appeal to those seeking stability in the jungles of current confusion.

Discipline for Inner Growth: Before you can be the stronger companion for another person, you must first accept your own weaknesses which need to be improved. Most of us know our basic weaknesses. Think about it positively now as something which can be overcome by singling out the person you know in your immediate circle who best portrays the opposite trait from your weakness. How does this person act in situations which frighten you? Can you go to that person and ask for the secret? If not, watch him quietly during the month of this discipline, and you may get a real clue to his display of courage which will help you become stronger.

Discipline for Outer Action: A basic rule for growth and making a habit automatic is to practice that habit consistently and frequently. Such an organization as Alcoholics Anonymous requires of its members that they help one another, being indeed companions in the fight to rebuild life. Therefore your inner growth may be equal to the amount of help you are willing to give others fighting their own battles. The exact handicap may not be the same as yours, but an essential weakness of a friend can be changed into power if the two of you promise to help each other face each day better. Find that friend and assure her of your sustaining prayers as she fights her battle, and let her know you are relying on hers for your own help.

Prayer: God, we are grateful that we are not left alone in this life, but that friends surround us who are often more willing to help than we are to ask for their fellowship. Beyond their ability to aid us lies divine help achievable through prayer for our personal needs. Stay with us daily as life's best heart companion. Amen.

16

Verse for Surmounting Scandal: "Draw me not away with the wicked, and with the workers of iniquity, which speak peace to their neighbors, but mischief is in their hearts."—Ps. 28:3

Seven Suggestions
for Surmounting Scandal

"I remember when there was all that scandal about her and that good-looking boy friend. This is exactly the way they said it happened. And that was twenty-five years ago next spring."

The woman who said this in my presence was beautifully gowned and freshly groomed. But it seemed to me as I looked at her across the teacups that her garments were soiled. I wanted to call her a "mental ghoul," as she dug into the buried sorrows and scandals of the past.

Sometimes it is easy for any of us to follow her bad example, adding to the problem of those involved in surmounting the scandalous circumstances. It is worth the effort it costs to keep from becoming part of this sharp-tongued group, because none of us knows when totally unexpected happenings may place us in the line of such open-fire discussions where our own loved ones may be concerned innocently.

Here are seven questions to ask yourself in determining whether you are slipping into that despicable group of people who thrive on scandal. Seven suggestions then show how to turn yourself around and become one of the pleasant people who help others forget their heartaches.

1. Am I more interested in the scandal of the past than the problems of the present? If so, maybe I should get to work trying to help the widow down on the corner by securing for her boy a scholarship to summer camp.

2. Do I ask the teller of tall tales to "tell me more" because I am avid for details of the rumor about the latest divorce in town? Then I should say instead, "I won't believe it until she tells me herself, and meanwhile I can hope it isn't true."

3. Do I get a vicarious thrill through reading the gory details of the latest sex murder as reported by the large dailies? Then maybe I should ask myself whether

I am showing enough love and affection to those who surround me in my own home.

4. Do I always have to know exactly how bloody the weekend traffic accident was, repeating endless details about how long it took to pry apart the tangled wreckage? Let us hope it will not take an accident to my own family car to show me how this exaggerated concern adds to the problems of those trying to care for the injured.

5. Do I try to delve into matters which are only the business of doctors and nurses when friends undergo surgery or encounter serious illness? Instead of repeating the fact that the right eye was torn out of its socket, I might spend the time in prayer that the specialist will be given ability to save the sight of the remaining eye.

6. Do I have to ferret out the financial facts in any tragedy and repeat that it is said that she had to mortgage the house to pay for the cancer illness and the funeral? Even if this is true, might I not better employ my time baking a loaf cake to take for the family's lunch?

7. Do I quote figures on how hard it is for the above forties to find a new job, if the husband of a friend is out of work? It takes no longer to comment on how capable is the job hunter, and watch his shoulders straighten as he begins again.

On the negative or positive answers to these seven guideposts depends much of the personal growth and happiness of the one who is being discussed. For the surrounding attitudes of his friends and acquaintances automatically begin to color the victim's response to tragedy and grief.

The good part about choosing to take the positive approach is that it is really easier than to wallow in the details of the sorrow or scandal. Once you learn the trick of dealing with compassion, a new world of fellowship opens for your heart.

For you come to see clearly that we each take our turn at experiencing situations which call for skill in coming out victorious. When we are the victims, we all cherish the one who comes to us with a cheerful approach, helping us work confidently toward a happy outcome.

When scandal or suspicious circumstances surround you, there are certain disciplines to put into immediate action for problem solving.

Discipline for Inner Growth: This involves learning the meaning of the word "empathy," which the dictionary defines as "imaginative projection of one's own consciousness into another being." Set aside ten minutes and sit down by yourself to contemplate the plight of the one currently involved with distressing circumstances in your circle. Stretch your imagination to see how you would want to be treated under such circumstances by asking such pertinent questions as these: Would I want to be left alone or to have companionship? Would I want people to talk about me or keep still? Would I want to know that my friends still cared about me? What factor would help me most to recover stability? By answering these queries honestly you will learn much about yourself and uncover strength for your future guidance when problems come into your life. You are also ready to help your friend by applying the technique most native to your own heart.

Discipline for Outer Action: Stop talking about a scandalous situation in your town, and do one specific positive thing to help solve some small part of the problem. The gesture may be an increased contribution to the Community Chest fund instead of criticism of its leaders mired down in a bad publicity campaign. It might involve asking your friendly social group to adopt the idea of a small western club which for a quarter of a century has contributed beautiful, handmade layettes to a home which helps unwed mothers.

Prayer: Father we have many blessings which can be spoiled by the thoughtless acts of others, not only in deed, but in word and attitude. Keep us from joining them by our illicit enjoyment of things which should be overlooked and forgotten. Teach us how to enter the hearts of others with such generous forgiveness of faults that we may all grow into clean citizenship. Amen.

17

Verse for Saving from Suicide: "We are troubled on every side, yet not distressed; we are perplexed, but not in despair."—II Cor. 4:8

Saving from Suicide

"Not until that tragic day when suicide actually happened in our own church did I ever give it more than a passing thought," said a church worker to her pastor.

Most of us share her feeling, and the deep regret at such tragic waste of time and talent. This is expressed well in the policy of the National Save-a-Life League, which says: "Suicide is a crime against man and a sin against God. Nearly everyone who resorts to it, as a final and public admission of failure, could be saved."

As the league points out, the impulse for self-destruction is found in the earliest history of man. The Old Testament tells of the death of King Saul, who deliberately fell upon his sword, and that of his servant who sought to kill King David and who later hanged himself. The Bible also gives the story of Zimri, who killed Elah, King of Israel, and then committed suicide by burning himself, and that of Judas Iscariot who hanged himself.

Against these four recorded examples of suicide in the Bible, there are many stories of those who rose above adversity, climaxing with the story of the crucified but risen Christ, who came into the world that the individual might have life, and life more abundant.

What are some of the underlying causes of suicide? Reports compiled by this league devoted to saving lives lists them as follows: unconfessed sin, loneliness, sickness, domestic trouble, financial loss. Automatically all who have tried suicide for these or other reasons and who come to the league are placed on a prayer list "committed to the care of our Heavenly Father."

The league maintains, for emergencies, a round-the-clock answering service which anyone can telephone at any hour of the day and night, assured that someone will listen to his deepest troubles. So much of the work of the trained counselors is just to sit and listen to problems that the league encourages individuals to learn the technique of listening to those

101

who may come to them with trouble in their own home, church, or community. They stress the often unexpected importance of simple friendly acts of kindness, and the power of a smile to help ward off discouragement.

Since suicide usually creates many more problems for those who are left, a part of the work of those who aid is in providing for the bereaved families. Perhaps a child needs the experience of summer camp with its opportunity to make new friends. It may be that a pair of shoes will enable him to keep on with school, or a coat will add to his self-respect.

Such little things are of greatest importance at a time when the innocent are trying to keep their own confidence in good repair. Sometimes something so small as a tiny headache pill will prevent the almost-suicide victim from proceeding with his plans. Professional counselors place great emphasis on so-called "small things."

They start by trying to get the intended victim to promise to postpone suicide for just one day. Workers believe that "it is a sin to hurl oneself at the judgment bar of God unbidden." If they can first talk the prospective victim into a definite promise to delay the act for twenty-four hours, they feel there is a chance for a complete victory.

Next, they ask for a simple promise to come to the office the next day for a visit. This gives the one who is melancholy something definite to look forward to within the next twenty-four hours. Also it assures him that someone will listen to his problem.

At first glance these seem such simple acts that it hardly seems possible the techniques could be important in saving lives. Yet the organization has an impressive record of a great number of lives saved in more than fifty years of outstanding service.

A surprising number of people in any community at some time contemplate self-destruction, as many pastors find out. Often it is the person who seems cheerful on the surface who confesses to a great burden within. So it becomes important for any alert individual to familiarize himself with ways to help in the event someone near him becomes depressed. Here are some simple steps which might save your own life, or that of a dear one.

Discipline for Inner Growth: Ask yourself a blunt question: How long has it been since anyone told me of his heartache? If it has been quite a while, do not make the mistake of assuming that the lives of all those near you are in "apple pie order." Perhaps you have let your own blessings make you smug and aloof. Resolve to listen quietly to the next problem brought to you. Then ask yourself a second question: How long has it been since I confided in anyone else? If you have forgotten how to let down the barriers, then you are on the way to becoming too self-sufficient.

Find a trusted confidante who will be available in time of great emergency.

Discipline for Outer Action: This involves preparation in order to be able to help when unexpected demands are made on your time and strength. Nobody likes to expect trouble, but there is nothing more frightening and frustrating than to be asked for help and not know where to turn. Therefore make now a contribution to a counseling service in your area, or send it to the National Save-A-Life League, 509 Fifth Avenue, New York, New York. Ask them for their folders concerning suicide prevention. Read these to bolster your own inherent wish to remain free from depression. Pass them along to a club leader, a Sunday-school teacher, or a friend who may with swift suddenness be in need of the ability to help a dear one.

Prayer: God, we accept so casually the great gift of life. Forgive us for ever becoming depressed when each day has much to offer if we keep our eyes open for its blessings. Comfort those who have lost the will to live, and restore them to patterns of usefulness. Keep us all in thy ever-loving care. Amen.

18

Verse for Defeating Gossip: "My tongue also shall talk of thy righteousness all the day long: for they are confounded, for they are brought unto shame, that seek my hurt."—Ps. 71:24

So They Say

"Remember, while they are talking about you, they are giving other people's troubles a rest." So said a wise older woman to a young woman who was the current victim of the gossips of the town. She herself had survived an onslaught of gossip several years before, and was now a respected member of the community, known for her gracious kindnesses.

Her advice did much to enable the young woman to walk the streets of her community even though she knew people were gossiping about a problem in her family circle which was distressing to her. There was a measure of relief in realizing that the circle of gossip goes round and round, and sooner or later someone else becomes the temporary victim. Gossiping now seems on a national and international basis, as well as over the back fence in countless small towns.

Columnists officially "peddle gossip" which is listened to eagerly by those who twirl radio or television dials. Much of this is sent out so far in advance of actual events that it cannot possibly be checked for accuracy. Instead, it is based on the flimsy foundation which is the creed of the gossip and which always begins, "so they say."

Perhaps gossip on any level serves chiefly as an escape mechanism from the pressing problems of the individual or the nation. It was explained by a husband that his wife "just talks and talks and talks." And when his friend wanted to know what the wife talked about, the husband answered, "She doesn't say."

This defines gossip, a constant talking and talking without bothering to ever say anything of real worth. Why, then, should gossip be allowed to hurt individual hearts so cruelly? For within any community there is almost always one person who has been so crippled emotionally by the talk of gossips that she is afraid to come out of her house and move freely among others. Haunted houses begin with haunted hearts, hurt by the hustlers of gossip. Often that "Queer old lady on the corner" was once the very attractive young girl about whom the gossips talked and talked.

Modern psychology provides some clues to help people meet the problems created by gossips. For psychologists say you can learn much about an individual's private fears and sins by listening to the type of subjects about which he gossips. Does the neighborhood racket-maker think the people next door are having marital trouble? Probably she feels insecure in her own marriage. Does the town snoop always think the worst of beautiful girls? Then she probably is resentful because she thinks she does not have the good looks of a sister or friend whom she pretends to love but secretly envies. Through gossip she tells the world about the skeletons in her own closet.

This may be small comfort to anyone who is being hurt by talk. How then shall the family which is being gossiped about react to the situation? Modern medicine says to face the problems honestly. If there is an element of truth on which the gossip is based, face this and take steps to see that it does not happen again. If the situation is being embroidered, then realize that emotions do hurt the body, so do not react in fury.

Always make a rational attempt to control anger and not act on impulse, even if this means delaying a mealtime until you are sufficiently recovered from the unjust remark to be able to eat without getting indigestion. Try to keep well physically so that the slurs and slights will not catch you with your bodily defenses lowered.

"Learn from the experience" is another good rule to follow. If the gossip is based on some activity in your life "on the shady side of the street," make a new effort to step out into the sunlight, where you cannot be so open to criticism. But if it is unfounded, try not to become embittered, and learn from those who are doing the talking just who are your real friends and who are fakes. Many a woman who has talked about a friend to her club members lives to wish she could call that same friend to come over and hold her own hand while she cries aloud over some unexpected blow which will be important to the town gossips.

Gossips usually end up lonely people, working hard at dredging up new bits to entice others. There are positive steps which can be taken to keep life interesting and defeat gossip.

Discipline for Inner Growth: This is a hard exercise, but it leads to the cultivating of spiritual strength which is of incalculable value in emergencies. For one whole day refuse to make any comment to anyone on the situation about which everyone is currently talking in your town. Anytime the subject is mentioned in your family circle, at the grocery store, after a church meeting, or while waiting in a dentist office, simply refuse to comment. Don't say anything. Remain silent. This is especially difficult if you happen to know some new fact which the other person is not yet telling.

But by refusing to speak, you gain the power to keep still when it is absolutely necessary to do so at some unexpected crisis in your life or that of your loved ones.

Discipline for Outer Action: It is as necessary to know when to speak out as it is to know how to keep silent. Particularly is this true if some cause in which you believe deeply is the unpopular side of a political argument at the moment. Sometimes gossip can be controlled by a constructive comment about municipal leaders, an accent on the good which is being accomplished by a minority group in its own welfare program, or an acceptance of some item in the program of a rival political party with whose broad concepts you are not in sympathy. Open your mouth and say one good thing about an individual involved in gossip, or an unpopular cause. This will help give you the strength of your convictions. It is one step to take you away from the dangerous habit of gossiping.

Prayer: Lord, we would remember whatsoever things are true, good, and just, and repeat them in our daily contacts. Guard the doors of our lips that we may make helpful comments and not the critical remarks which hurt and destroy. We thank thee for thy words of life. Amen.

19

Verse for Accepting Sympathy: "He that goeth forth and weepeth, bearing precious seed, shall doubtless come again with rejoicing, bringing his sheaves with him."—Ps. 126:6

Accepting Sympathy

"Sometimes I think the hardest part of this tragic situation is having to accept the sympathy of others." A dear friend made this remark to me in the middle of a family catastrophe.

Yet the time comes to almost all families when they must learn how to accept sympathy. For many this represents a real problem in growth and understanding.

Why should it be so hard for most of us to accept

110

sympathy? After all, we offer sympathy to others, and expect them to accept our best intentions. Paradoxically we sometimes almost refuse to accept it when the circle comes full turn to us.

Sympathy may be offered into our lives for many reasons—loss of a job, death of a loved one, chronic ill health of a child, or damage to a home through fire or flood.

Complicating the original problem which prompts the offer of solicitude is the fact that the individual does not understand the technique of accepting gracefully the well-meant efforts of others.

Perhaps because of pride, we are unwilling to admit that this special set of circumstances surrounds us. We had thought we would be above the need for sympathy from our fellows. We knew other people sometimes needed it, but we didn't think this would happen in our family circle.

Furthermore it seems that any other trial would be better than this particular one. Surely that situation in our neighbor's life which causes him pain would be much easier to face than the one which has been dumped unceremoniously into our midst.

This resentment over facts must first be removed. If we take a good straight look at the circumstances, probably we will be able to concede that it certainly appears to others as though an expression of sympathy might be in order, and even expected.

111

Then if they are kind enough to offer sympathy, the least we can do is to reach out our hands to accept what they bring. Immediately there is the possibility of a new emotional problem, for once sympathy is accepted, there is the danger of wanting to take too much of it into the heart to comfort the rough spots of living. If we accept too much from our friends, this will turn the mind inward to self-pity.

Therefore the advice of a woman who has surmounted much helps to give the proper balance. She says, "Take just enough sympathy to help you get a better grip on your load." This defines the problem of the one who gives and the one who receives.

Essentially sympathy is offered to try to help us bear the load which, for one reason or another, life has brought to our hearts. Accepting offered sympathy without cringing may serve to make that load lighter. It may show us the best way to offer our own sympathy to others when they in turn face their problems.

A side effect to the offer of sympathy, particularly at time of death, is the fear of weeping during the exchange. Somehow the myth has grown up that it is wrong to shed tears. The opposite is true, however, and in their shedding there may be a real release of emotion and tension. What are tear ducts for if not to wash away dust from the eyes and help us see more clearly?

The most effective piece of sympathy witnessed in

one community was that when an elderly preacher was conducting the final rites for a beloved neighborhood "grandma." It had been a long and wasting illness, and death came as a blessed release. Yet many remained to mourn her, and miss her wise counsel.

The preacher stood before the group with his sermon notes and the psalms to read for comfort. As he began the brief obituary he suddenly stopped in mid-sentence and said simply, "I have lost a friend and I feel lonely without her. I will have to try hard to find someone else to pick up the prayer load she carried for me."

He lifted his hand to his face and wiped away a tear. Then he took out his white pocket-handkerchief and wiped it across his eyes. In the knowledge that someone was weeping with them, the family found strength and comfort, and was able to accept sympathy.

Certain steps are involved in the exchange of tactful gestures of sympathy, and these can be cultivated by anyone.

Discipline for Inner Growth: Turn out the light and sit alone in the dark with your thoughts for fifteen minutes of meditation on the situation closest to you calling for sympathetic concern on your part. Use as the basis of your thinking the shortest verse of the Bible, "Jesus wept." Reflect on what this means in a sophisticated generation, and how it promises companionship in any sad situation. How can you accept such divine aid if you have forgotten how to receive from those who live in the same house with you, or your neighbors or friends? Begin your mental recovery by seeing that if the tragedy has made you humble enough to receive sympathy, then there are blessings ahead.

Discipline for Outer Action: You must accept the first gesture which is made to you, whether it is the act of a stranger in opening the door at a market, your husband's offer to pick up a package at the laundry, or the scraggly bouquet of wild flowers brought to the door by a child. Do not refuse any offer of help, no matter how small, and no matter how well you are able to do the same act for yourself. Learn in good days how to accept little acts of kindness so that your heart will be stretched large enough to accept sympathy when deep sorrow comes close and threatens to engulf your mind and energies. This time let the other fellow do for you, while you repay him with a simple "Thank you."

Prayer: God who yearned over Jerusalem, forgive us for turning away from thy love because we have forgotten how to accept the concern of others. Strip away the artificial layers of brittleness so that we will not be afraid to face our own emotions. Give us grace to accept that we may learn how better to give. Amen.

20

Verse for Overcoming Hurts: "For I will restore health unto thee, And I will heal thee of thy wounds, saith the Lord."—Jer. 30:17

Soothing Hurt Feelings

On the happy Sunday morning when Bibles were to be presented to children who had completed third-grade work, the Sunday-school pupils filed into the church service. Proudly the pupils sat with their teacher in the front pew while the superintendent called the names.

As he read from a list, probably prepared by another person, one by one the children went forward to receive their Bibles. Shyly, but with anticipated pleasure based on weeks of study, they smiled happily as they returned to their seats.

I watched them go forward in careful order until the superintendent came to the little girl in the pink ruffled dress whose blonde pony tail was secured with blue barrettes in the shape of tiny hats. The children on either side of her went up for their Bibles, and I thought she must be sitting out of place alphabetically. But no, when the list was completed, her name still had not been read. Then the little girl in pink began to cry, rubbing the back of her hands into her eyes and trying to keep the tears from showing. Her teacher moved closer to put a comforting arm around her.

All through the sermon I wondered how the teacher would handle this so that the little girl would not feel hurt and permanently discouraged in her attitude toward Sunday school and church. But when the service was over, the problem became even more complicated. Irate parents descended upon the teacher and superintendent, demanding an explanation. The mother's voice could be heard shrilly criticizing all in the department.

Finally it was the little girl herself who made the first move toward reconciliation. She went over to the superintendent and asked him a question. Whereupon he showed her the list and she realized her name had not been put on it for some reason.

Then he asked her a question and she nodded

vehemently "yes," which apparently meant she had satisfactorily finished the work. As they came closer toward me, the superintendent asked the girl a second question, and I realized he must have asked her for forgiveness for the oversight. For she hesitated a second and then said, "Yes, I will, it's all right now."

Next the teacher spoke to her, and I heard the little girl say, "I'm sorry I cried in church." The teacher said that sometimes he felt like crying himself, even if he were older and bigger. The little girl swished by me toward her playmates, the ruffles swinging on her perky dress, and I felt sure she would be in Sunday school next week. But I was not so certain about her parents, for adults seem to find it more difficult to soothe their own hurt feelings. Sometimes they let matters drag on without taking prompt action to change the picture.

In this case, the superintendent and teacher together had taken immediate steps to determine if a mistake had been made, and to try to show the child that it was not intended. Otherwise, the child might have felt that her efforts to persevere had been of no use, and her fellow students might have caught this attitude from her.

Now at least all the boys and girls knew that the teacher and superintendent were trying hard to do the right thing. They had seen that sometimes both adults and children have to ask forgiveness and try again. We live in a world where unintended slights are bound to occur.

The important thing is to see that the breach is not allowed to widen, but that early steps are taken to heal the wounds of the heart. This involves honestly facing hurt feelings and not saying defensively, "She couldn't possibly hurt me." This is usually an admission that the hurt has gone deep.

The second step involves the realization that the one who seemingly inflicted the slight may also have been caught in circumstances not of his own choosing. Perhaps he was following through on insufficient evidence or taking on himself the failure of a fellow worker. Since blame cannot be accurately assessed, perhaps censure should not be allowed to complicate the act of forgiveness.

Involve the smallest number of persons in the slight and there are the fewest feelings to consider when starting over again. The doctors tell us that each of us has our own personal threshold of pain, and this is true of hurt feelings. There are ways whereby we can build more healthy and stable feelings.

Discipline for Inner Growth: Ask yourself whether as the years go by you become more sensitive or less sensitive to real or fancied hurts. Do your feelings need to be soothed with the balm of special

119

consideration more often now than five years ago? Do you create this situation by the attitudes you take toward others? Have you allowed the whims of your own ego to become so great that you expect others to cater to these needs constantly? A few hurt feelings may be good for you, showing clearly the areas of your life which need to be improved. Any person who feels secure does not allow others to shake his confidence by small slights. Time saved from apologies and repairs to hurt feelings can be invested in productive living.

Discipline for Outer Action: Set the record straight between you and the last person who hurt your feelings. This may not need words, but it does mean that you must stop avoiding the individual involved. Recognize that he may not even know about your hurt feelings. Seek the first opportunity to meet that person face to face in a tearoom or at the grocery store, and say a civil word about the weather. Your own strength grows if you take such initiative. It is never a sign of weakness to make the first move, but a proof that your own feelings are coming under your own control.

Prayer: Father, forgive us the wasted energy expended in keeping our hurt feelings in repair. Help us visualize what could be accomplished for thee if we kept our emotions in check and did not have to be treated like babies. Let us grow in grace toward our fellows, and so accept more fully thine own grace generously granted us. Amen.

21

*Verse for Money Wisdom: "Wherefore
do ye spend money for that which is not bread?
and your labour for that which satisfieth not? hearken
diligently unto me, and eat ye that which
is good, and let your soul delight
itself in fatness."—Isa. 55:2*

Money Squabbles

"Do you mean you can pay without fussing?" A little girl in a jaunty red coat and white cap asked this in my hearing the other day. Her family was considering going to a restaurant for a birthday dinner. Someone said it would be simple to pay for the party in advance at the time the place cards and flowers were placed on the table. This would leave the entire evening free for just plain family talk and relaxing.

Entranced, the child listened eagerly to these details. When asked for an explanation of her question, she said she had always supposed that talking about who paid for the piece of paper the waitress left was a part of eating out at a restaurant. She had watched the quarters and dollars and dimes being divided when the amount was tallied among the various members.

"It takes so much time," she said, "sometimes I almost forget what I had to eat." This child had actually worried about whether there was money enough to pay the bill. If there had been any question of lack of finances, naturally the family would not have planned the affair in the first place.

Far from being a happy experience, the restaurant meal had made the child tense and filled with uncertainty. This had not been confined to elaborate meals, for often there had been as much fussing at the hamburger stand.

Her remark showed the family that just by cutting out the "fussing" adults can help a child to cultivate a sense of security. Discarding the habit of arguing over details may even improve the appetites of the adults, who also suffer from squabbles.

In a world which becomes increasingly tense with fears involving hydrogen and atom bombs, sometimes it seems there is little that adults can do to help children achieve a sense of stability. Living with these weapons involves talk about how much they cost and where will funds be found sufficient for defense needs, and this aggravates a child's sense of money need.

When money squabbles are conducted on a national scale, adults themselves become confused. Anger over mounting taxes adds to the general resentment over money problems. It seems too simple to think that by refusing to squabble over a restaurant check any progress could be made, but this can help a child find his way to better emotional security where finances are concerned.

For essentially, all squabbles contribute to a feeling of frustration. A child comes to think that money is completely unmanageable, as indeed it sometimes turns out to be when he begins to handle his own allowance. He tries the technique of fussing when he wants more than he can afford to buy, and thinks he can wheedle additional funds. Often he is silenced by gifts so the squabbles remain minor. Great conflict later develops with sometimes tragic consequences if he still feels he should have more than his family ultimately can provide. A badly motivated child may steal to fill this lack. Stopping the money squabbles at the beginning can curb this later tendency and may avoid this form of delinquency.

Are there rules which can be followed to change the pattern of squabbling? One wise retired banker, rich in advice to leaders of community drives, has a personal law of finance by which he lives. He advises its use in churches and clubs. The rule can be adapted to money squabbles at all ages in life. The philosophy of this wise man is summed up in one sentence.

"Always estimate your expenses at a maximum and your income at a minimum," he says. By following this rule, if the expenses run less, there is a balance. If the income runs more, there is still a balance. To reverse the use of the words maximum and minimum invariably leads to trouble.

Such advice runs contrary to most current spending, from national governments to small municipalities. It is also true that church groups end up with deficits because the idea was not followed. Surely the money squabbles of organizations become more involved than the plaintive and wistful request of the small child hoping to avoid confusion.

An individual can learn certain disciplines concerning money management, which lead to peace of mind and greater usefulness.

Discipline for Inner Growth: Stop thinking about what you do not have, and start concentrating on the abundance which is already in your possession. This calls for a complete change in the thinking pattern of most adults, for we live in an age of "gimmes"—give me this, give me that, and then give me some more. Each day you practice this discipline, you must add mentally to the list of things you already possess. In this period do not buy anything new, but give a fresh use to an old object. The chipped pitcher may be the perfect vase for the bright zinnias. You don't need a new picture for the hall so much as to change the faded one for the bright photograph back in the closet full of vacation souvenirs.

Discipline for Outer Action: Life must be kept fluid and flexible for happiness, and this law applies to money matters as well. If you fail temporarily in your wish to feel financially secure, then force yourself to make some monetary gift to someone who needs it worse than you do. Releasing your mind from the tension of selfishness will enable you to spend your energy looking for a better job or concentrating so well on your current task that you may receive a promotion. Make a gift to a community charity or church mission project—with no prospect of tangible return—for this will remind you anew of spiritual blessings. Those who tithe testify to the expanding power of the money which remains after the first tenth is returned to God.

Prayer: God, we live in a world of wants, and sometimes we forget that what we want most is an increasing knowledge of thy presence. Speak to us above the clamor of coins that we may be led out of confusion. Help us to be aware each day of the abundance of thy goodness. Amen.

22

Verse for Making Choices: "A good man out of the good treasure of the heart bringeth forth good things: and an evil man out of the evil treasure bringeth forth evil things."—Matt. 12:35

Do You Trick or Treat Yourself?

"Trick or treat!" Clearly the three words sound on the night air as children arrive on Halloween. The way seems quite simple to them. Specific choice is plainly offered.

One way lies good conduct. The other way lies bad. There is no hazy compromise in between. Every once in a while it is a good idea for adults to look at their own actions, and say clearly the three words which define decision, "Trick or treat!"

Sometimes a survey of current situations will show that the heart is tricking itself, when it would be as easy and better to treat.

Do you worry about the past that cannot be changed? Then you are tricking yourself out of the happiness of the present. You might as well treat yourself to a pleasant future by making the most of today.

Do you keep your mind filled with the unpleasant things which happened, perhaps the clerk who seemed rude to you? Then you are tricking yourself down the path of resentment which leads to misery. You might as well start treating yourself by remembering the times when you have been served well.

Do you fear that your health will not hold up to your daily routine demands of earning a living or taking care of the home? Then you are tricking yourself by adding that most debilitating of emotions—fear—to the hazards of your health. Why not treat yourself to the energy which comes from attacking physical problems with faith in the ultimate outcome for good?

Do you feel alone and friendless, and think nobody loves you anymore? Then you are tricking yourself down the long road of selfishness and concern for your own feelings. Why not treat yourself to the pleasure of making a new friend by telephoning someone and inviting that person in for coffee and an hour of conversation and fellowship?

Do you think the world itself is getting more shallow and perverse each day? Then you are tricking yourself into a feeling of failure about the world at large. You might better treat yourself to a new vision of what you can do to make the world better, perhaps by volunteering to serve on one of the welfare boards of your community.

Do the young people bother you so that you think the next generation will not be able to pick up the problems it inherits from this one? Then you are tricking yourself into negative thinking which may contribute to creating such problems. Far better to treat yourself to the joy of coming to know some young person by speaking to the teenager who is washing his automobile down the street.

"Trick or treat" sounds so deceptively simple, just a handy phrase to use for requesting a handout at the door. Yet properly applied this same phrase can determine the gifts which life itself hands out to the heart which knocks at the doorway of good living.

Every once in awhile it is a good idea to stop to decide whether you are expecting your personality to trick or treat your life with its problems and opportunities.

This involves learning how to make choices. One good way to do this is to take two sheets of paper and list on one all of the reasons for a project, and on the other to list all the reasons against this same project. You may think you have the matter well in mind, but putting it down in black and white helps clarify the issue.

Then by the process of elimination you will be able to see the valid reasons which remain for taking action for or against the issue. If you have too many negative reasons, indicating your fear about starting a project, it may well be that you have already fallen into the dangerous habit of tricking yourself out of success.

If, after counting up the reasons for going ahead, the project seems unworthy of your efforts, it can be abandoned. Or it may seem more desirable than ever to accomplish your goal. There are ways to learn how to treat yourself far more times than you are tricked if you apply certain disciplines to your goals and conduct.

Discipline for Inner Growth: If you wish to develop along positive lines, it is first necessary to establish a climate for the growth of constructive ideas. This involves removing temporarily any restrictive bonds of rejection or revision of ideas. Let yourself have the fun this minute of imagining exactly what you would be doing if you could do exactly what you wanted to be doing. This is not as obvious at it sounds. You must first form a picture of your dreams, and most of us keep our goals so haphazard that it is hard to pictorialize any specific situation. Do this now without wondering how or when your dream could possibly be brought into being. Grow within your heart by taking a good look at what you want most.

Discipline for Outer Action: Take the first small step toward realizing that dream. Do you want to go to Australia by jet airplane? Then stop by a travel agency and pick up a folder and saturate yourself with colored pictures of the plane and area to be visited. Do you want to buy a jeep for a missionary friend? Then pick up the folders telling of its mechanical qualifications and find out the price. Drop these realistic facts into your mind and let your subconscious go to work on them. You will be surprised at the suggestions which will come to you shortly about how to plan your vacation, or where to secure funds for the mission gift. You must first do one thing which will treat yourself into final victory, and not continue to trick yourself into thinking the dream cannot be accomplished.

Prayer: Father, we believe that thy plans for us are greater than our ability to comprehend. Keep us from standing in our own light. Help us to get out of our muddled thinking by accepting once and for all the fact that we are meant for life, and life more abundant. Amen.

23

Verse for Stability: "And the peace of God, which passeth all understanding, shall keep your hearts and minds through Christ Jesus."—Phil. 4:7

Just Being There

"He likes to know I am there. Just being there seems to help him."

The wife of a man facing long hospitalization gave this as her reason for making daily trips to the hospital.

No, there wasn't anything she could do for him. The nurses took care of his physical wants, the doctor ordered the diet and medicines.

He wasn't able to read any magazines she might bring. Indeed, he didn't want her to read to him. The time came ultimately when he was so spent he didn't even want to talk about life outside.

Yet he liked to have her there, just in the room with him. From this he seemed to draw the strength which ultimately brought about his recovery, to the great surprise of everyone.

"Just being there" is in the last analysis all that any of us can ever do for those we love. Maybe we can't see any way out of the current difficulty with which a dear friend is involved, but at least we can be standing by, and let her know we are there hoping the solution will present itself.

It may be that the knowledge that even one other person wants to help could furnish the individual with sufficient strength to enable him to make a fresh start.

Nor does it matter if this is a physical ailment or an emotional hurt or a financial loss. There is unsuspected power when two people face a difficult situation together.

For the example of their devotedness can rally other friends to their sides. It can turn someone else far removed from this particular situation, and who is discouraged, to a new realization that because others are trying to solve their problems, he should gird himself better for the facing of his own.

Perhaps you know someone now who needs a fresh assurance that you are standing by in friendship, or as a member of the family, or even as a fellow human being in the same community, involved in the great task of building a decent life.

If you are separated by distance and can't be there in person, you can send a note of encouragement through the mail. When you can't find the words to write in a note, you can always offer up a prayer. Keep your heart open with the willingness to be there and to aid in any way possible.

Such aid cannot be offered unless the individual who is standing by makes frequent efforts to keep his own "battery recharged." You cannot continue to give out unless you arrange to take in fresh sources of energy.

This means deliberately cultivating happy experiences when away from the sickroom. Go for a walk around the hospital grounds and breathe in deeply of the good, fresh air, away from the smells of medicine inside. Can you find a yellow daisy in the grass, or a bird's nest on the branch of a tree?

Do not keep a morbid sense of guilt because you are free to go out to dinner while the patient remains behind with hospital food. Find some place with a homey atmosphere, or a foreign restaurant which will give your mind fresh horizons to think about. Then you can take a new, relaxed point of view back to the sickroom when you return in the evening.

Explore the area to see where the nearest church is located. This does not need to be one of your own faith. Perhaps you will find a large metropolitan church which is open for prayer. Maybe it will be a small and almost deserted and forgotten neighborhood church. If the pastor is at work on some report or his sermon, he will not mind if you sit alone in the shadow of the red, stained-glass window. Rest while away from the constant commotion of being around people at the hospital.

Walking is one of the best restorers of mental and spiritual balance to those involved in conflict and crisis. You owe it to yourself to keep the physical body in as good shape as possible so you can face up to the demands of the emergency. No good will come to your beloved patient if your own strength ebbs too low.

Being there with someone implies that you are also wise enough to be alone with your God, restoring your own strength, so that you have the more to give to those in need. There are many ways to strengthen yourself so you can keep on "being there."

Discipline for Inner Growth: Open your New Testament and begin to read it, not a chapter at a time, but going on into the next chapter, and the one beyond that, for as long as you have time between errands. Just read the words and let them fall into your tired brain and worried heart. Don't try to comprehend their theological or philosophical meaning in your hour of distress. Permit the words of life to come

135

into your own heart and work their miracle for you by gradually giving you strength and confidence and faith. You will find that pertinent, powerful phrases will come back to you which you can repeat silently while you sit by the bedside, or which will come to your lips when a friend begs for help.

Discipline for Outer Action: Walk into the nearest bookstore and secure a pocket-size copy of a New Testament or book of Psalms to keep with you at all times. Promise yourself to carry it with you and to read it often for strength to help in this current crisis. Don't be embarrassed at opening it to read under a beauty parlor hair dryer, even though you have never done this before. Keep your promise by reading it while waiting for a tire to be changed or gasoline to be put into your automobile. Such reading of Scripture openly will bring you many unexpected and surprising comments from those who serve you on these routine errands. Many will volunteer which passages have helped them most, and you will discover anew how much you have missed by neglecting such reading in good days.

Prayer: Father, how glad we are that you do not go away and leave us alone to face our problems. Fundamentally we know that thou art always there, more willing to help than we are to ask. Give us inner stability to stand by those who need the knowledge that human friendship is also available in life's trials. Amen.

24

Verse for Waiting: "But they that wait
upon the Lord shall renew their strength;
they shall mount up with wings as eagles; they
shall run, and not be weary; and they shall
walk, and not faint."—Isa. 40:31

Sit Tight and Wait

Whenever a new freeway route is an-
nounced, the advice to those who live nearby is given
as "sit tight and wait." This is hard to accept, for
the building of new roads calls for the taking of certain property which may for many years have been
used for residences or public buildings.

Surveying the best and exact route sometimes takes
many months, stretching into years. Even after the

best route is announced, it takes a long time to complete all the legal details and get the property on which to build.

Meanwhile there is a normal tendency to panic as residents in old-time areas hear that the freeway is soon to move through their property. Old associations will be swept away, they fear, and they hurry to find a new place, perhaps with as many disadvantages as the older site. It has happened that some who hurried have had to scurry out of the way of new freeways as many as three times because of hasty decisions to move.

Far from wishing they had sold, some other old-timers find themselves glad to welcome the progress brought into their lives by the final appearance of the freeway. "I'm so thankful we waited" becomes the theme song of those who accepted the advice of being patient, even under protest.

In facing any change, most of us have a tendency to become inwardly panicky and to try to run away from facing what is about to disturb the normal pattern of our lives. None of us wants to accept the easy advice to "sit tight and wait."

Yet in this advice is much good for the facing of any difficult problem, as the experience of those involved with the materialistic building of new roads indicates. The four words "sit tight and wait" are the modern equivalent of the old-fashioned urging to "remember to have patience."

However it may be phrased in different generations, this is a practical virtue which can keep the individual from making headstrong mistakes. If he can remain settled enough to wait when problems appear in life, he can find that there is often value in waiting.

This is not to be confused with procrastination. Active waiting involves knowing that you are deliberately standing still while the forces of life attempt to push you in many directions, none of which appears to be the right one at the moment. Perhaps standing still is a solution which has not appeared to others, but as the shifting circumstances change, your own stance will seem now to be the one which is right for you.

Waiting with awareness of the current problems is very different than just "waiting for something to turn up." It means that you know clearly the advantages and disadvantages of your current position, and that you want to be sure that any move has definite blessings as well as the ability to take you away from the depressing factors in your present surroundings.

Running away from the problems of life always brings in its wake new problems, which call for extra resources in solving. At least all your strength can be focused on the original problem if you remain still enough to work at it with all your heart and might to find the solution. Perhaps someone who tried to hurt you will have his own new problems, and you will see how minor is the situation into which you were plunged, and which at first seemed so severe.

There are always many unexpected factors such as the sudden death of a business leader, discovery of a new product in your line of sales, or changing techniques of management brought about by moving into the space age. These factors both for sorrow and joy change the position of your own problem, even though you remain in the same spot physically.

If, after all the evidence is gathered, you still feel a change is for the better, then you are the one who is the master of the situation. You are not being shoved around by factors not of your own choosing, but make the move of your own volition, having considered it in the process of waiting. Now your energies can be focused on the future without being dissipated in thoughts of the past and lost in regrets of what might have been accomplished before changes were demanded.

Waiting is never an easy task, but it can be made easier by the adoption of certain attitudes to bring your dreams into reality.

Discipline for Inner Growth: Stop your hurrying, and practice moving more slowly in your daily tasks. Say to yourself, "All my huffing and puffing will not blow this problem away." Try to see the total situation as though it were a slow-motion picture passing before your eyes. Remember how jerky the movements are when film is speeded up? Probably you will look as grotesque to yourself in later years if you persist on rushing through this situation. Listen to a favorite piece of music, and note how much harmony and sweetness is added by moments of rest, the quiet pauses in the melody. Waiting now can make all your future more beautiful, if you do it with a heart trusting in God's goodness.

Discipline for Outer Action: Prove that you are learning how to wait positively by convincing those closest to you of your inner attitude of patience and hopefulness. Do this by daily speaking cheerfully about the future, and avoiding any fearful comments involving worry or doubt. Make a definite list of all the good and needed factors which have already come into being, and also list precisely what is still needed to make the waiting period a thing of the past. Give thanks for the appearance of each new blessing. This "active waiting," which involves the complete surrender of your present to God, will give you increasing confidence that he is even now making ready the abundance of your future.

Prayer: God, whenever life asks us to wait, we become restless and impatient in this speeded-up world. Forgive us for hurting any of thy children through our resentment and our unwillingness to adjust happily to thy time-plan for our lives. Take care of our dreams, and give us the assurance of thy eternal companionship. Amen.